Loose Pages

PRAISE FOR
WHAT DRIVES YOU

This is not just another book. It's a course in living with purpose, conviction, and influence. Be prepared for challenging questions that force you to see much of your life as default from your history, family expectations, and cultural tradition. Background, genetics, and nurture weigh heavily in how we are living today, but we all have choices for creating our future. This book is a wealth of information drawn from the introspective interviews of the world's top experts gathered by one of the top interviewers in the world today.

> —**Dan Miller,** author of *48 Days to the Work You Love*

Kevin Miller takes us on a deep dive inward, asking us to tune out all the hype that surrounds us and to ask the questions that get to the heart of our most reliable resource—our energy and motivation. Let this book guide you to a clearer sense of what your life is about, and what it can become.

> —**Dr. Robert Waldinger,** professor of psychiatry,
> Harvard Medical School, and *New York Times*
> bestselling author of *The Good Life*

I have a core belief that love doesn't have to be earned or found, it has to be realized. Kevin's book beautifully refutes the myth that being driven is similarly found, but showcases it is simply and profoundly realized when you audit yourself for what you truly value and desire. Just like with love, our drive is unique and glorious. I urge you to let Kevin guide you to finding love and fulfillment in your authentic drive.

> —**Humble The Poet,** Canadian-born rapper, spoken-word
> artist, poet, and internationally bestselling author of
> *How to Be Loved*

I've spent decades as a professional communicator through different mediums, first as a Broadway and film actress in the entertainment industry, and now as a professional communication coach helping people communicate in life and business. Therefore, I value a book that communicates clearly and powerfully. In Kevin's book, he has masterfully communicated the essence of drive in a way I feel has never been done before. He gets to the root issue of what drives us and lays it out simply. By reading the book, you'll be forever altered in understanding how and why you're driven. This book is a must-read to add to your professional and self-development toolbox.

—**Renée Marino,** actress Mary Delgado in Clint Eastwood's *Jersey Boys*, professional communication coach/TEDx speaker, and bestselling author of *Becoming a Master Communicator*

Brilliant! Kevin Miller's *What Drives You* describes exactly what you can do to fill the void so you can live full out. *What Drives You* is a go-to road map to becoming a more joyful and fulfilled person. Read this book and become the person you've always wanted to become and help others do the same.

—**Richie Norton,** bestselling author of *Anti-Time Management*

Kevin has a brilliant understanding of the difference between people who know how to stay motivated and those who struggle to keep their inner drive engaged in a healthy way. We like to think success stories are just outliers and special cases, but the truth is anyone can have a fulfilling, happy life that uplifts you and everyone around you when you know what lifts you up energetically. This book is a great explanation of how we can lift ourselves up, stay up, and achieve our dreams.

—**Ken Honda,** Japan's #1 self-help guru and bestselling author of *Happy Money*

Are you seeking the spark or the catalyst that unlocks your full potential? *What Drives You* is the rare key that helps unlock your potential not just for success, but for fulfillment. This book will get more out of you so you can get more out of life.

—**Tom Ziglar,** CEO, Zig Ziglar Corp.

I began life with no apparent drive. Then I discovered what I valued, and my life changed, bringing me to where I am now. This is why Kevin used my story in *What Drives You*. What he guides you through is what will ignite the strong drive you've always desired. A drive that takes you where you want to go with confidence and peace. Put this book at the front of your bookshelf, as your drive is the fuel for everything you dream of doing.

—**Lori Harder,** bestselling author, top podcaster,
investor, and multi-passionate entrepreneur

In his book, *What Drives You*, Kevin Miller has written something that is both deeply philosophical and immensely practical. It is frightening, in a really good way, and can be a great source of peace for those who want to live lives of meaning and purpose. I honestly can't imagine anyone who would not benefit from reading this and putting it into practice.

—**Patrick Lencioni,** bestselling author of
The Five Dysfunctions of a Team
and *The Six Types of Working Genius*

From the first time I was a guest on Kevin's podcast, I resonated with his insight into my messages and his desire to authentically uncover what really helps us achieve personal growth. This book is an incredible map to guide you to uncover and clarify what you truly value and care about for your life, which is what drive is. Kevin covers age-old wisdom in a truly unique and relatable methodology anyone will greatly benefit from.

> —**Dr. Benjamin Hardy,** organizational psychologist and
> bestselling author of *Be Your Future Self Now*

Everyone is enamored with habits, but having good habits assumes you have the core motives and drive to create, implement, and sustain them. *What Drives You* is really the prequel to habits, as it helps you establish your why, which is what actually drives what you will and won't ever do. This book should be required reading for anyone desiring to actually improve themselves.

> —**Jordan Harbinger,** host of *The Jordan Harbinger Show*
> podcast

Anyone who knows or listens to Kevin Miller's podcast knows he's driven—driven to help his audience members grow and thrive. Now he invites us to discover what drives us. Reading this book, you might be surprised: It's not always what you think. If you want to put yourself back in the driver's seat of your own life, you need this book.

> —**Michael Hyatt,** founder and chairman, Full Focus,
> and bestselling author of *Your Best Year Ever*

WHAT DRIVES YOU

YOU

How to Discover Your Unique
Motivators and *Accelerate Growth*
in Work and Life

KEVIN MILLER

New York Chicago San Francisco Athens London Madrid
Mexico City Milan New Delhi Singapore Sydney Toronto

1 2 3 4 5 6 7 8 9   LCR   28 27 26 25 24 23

ISBN   978-1-264-26976-1
MHID   1-264-26976-5

e-ISBN 978-1-264-26977-8
e-MHID   1-264-26977-3

Library of Congress Cataloging-in-Publication Data

Names: Miller, Kevin A.,- author.
Title: What drives you : how to discover your unique motivators and
    accelerate growth in work and life / Kevin Miller.
Description: 1 Edition. | New York : McGraw Hill, [2023] | Includes
    bibliographical references and index.
Identifiers: LCCN 2022058683 (print) | LCCN 2022058684 (ebook) |
    ISBN 9781264269761 (hardback) | ISBN 9781264269778 (ebook)
Subjects: LCSH: Self-actualization (Psychology) | Happiness. | Success.
Classification: LCC BF637.S4 M54835 2023 (print) | LCC BF637.S4
    (ebook) | DDC 158.1—dc23/eng/20230313
LC record available at https://lccn.loc.gov/2022058683
LC ebook record available at https://lccn.loc.gov/2022058684

McGraw Hill books are available at special quantity discounts to use as premiums and sales promotions or for use in corporate training programs. To contact a representative, please visit the Contact Us pages at www.mhprofessional.com.

McGraw Hill is committed to making our products accessible to all learners. To learn more about the available support and accommodations we offer, please contact us at accessibility@ mheducation.com. We also participate in the Access Text Network (www.accesstext.org), and ATN members may submit requests through ATN.

This book is dedicated to:

All those who question how much drive they really have.
You have access to all you need. Right now.
You're about to learn this truth.

The very driven individuals. My people. But who may
be frustrated in some areas of their lives where they are
driving hard and not getting the results they want. And
missing some peace. I get you. You'll find solace here.

My kids, who were the catalyst for this book. I hope and
pray you find what you want and enjoy the drive more
than the destinations. I'm always here, you never have
to drive alone except for when . . . you need to.

My wife, who has borne the greatest brunt of my often
erratic and errant driving. Thanks for sticking it out.
We've enjoyed some great, glorious destinations. I'm
eternally grateful for you and expecting many more.

CONTENTS

Introduction   ix

PART ONE
DRIVING SCHOOL

CHAPTER 1   Being Driven Is Just a Thought Away   3

CHAPTER 2   Unlocking Your Unique Drive   21

PART TWO
DRIVING LESSONS

CHAPTER 3   What Drives Your Purpose:
You Are What You Have Faith In   47

CHAPTER 4   What Drives Your Relationships:
You Are Who You Love   71

CHAPTER 5   What Drives Your Body:
You Are How You Look and Feel   101

CHAPTER 6   What Drives Your Mind:
You Are How You Think and Feel   129

CHAPTER 7   **What Drives Your Work:**
You Are What You Do   **153**

CHAPTER 8   **What Drives Your Money:**
You Are What You Have and Don't Have   **177**

CHAPTER 9   **What Drives Your Achievements:**
You Are What You've Achieved   **201**

PART THREE

VICTORY LAP

CHAPTER 10   **Driving Mastery**   **227**

Acknowledgments   **239**

Notes   **243**

Index   **247**

Drive: a very strong energy and determination to achieve a goal or satisfy a need

INTRODUCTION

The Reason for This Book

It was early on a Saturday morning before the rest of my family was awake, but late enough that the sun was streaming through the windows of our home high in the Colorado Rocky Mountains. In this season I had gotten into a habit of taking these mornings to ponder my own life lessons and impart them to some of my adult children. This particular morning, following some deep conversations over the previous week with high-profile influencers on my podcast, I was simply thinking past the normal platitudes of self-help and thinking about what I really wanted for my kids. The answer? I wanted them to be good people who benefited other humans and, ultimately, felt fulfilled and at peace. That's when it hit me. That last word, *peace*, might be what I most wanted for them, but I didn't have much of it. While I'd achieved a good amount and truly had a lot of fulfillment, I had recently experienced my first true encounter with burnout—and was about to face even more.

Legendary baseball coach Yogi Berra was once driving with his family to the Baseball Hall of Fame, and his wife, Carmen, was giving him a hard time about being lost. Yogi replied, "We're lost. But we're making good time!" From early childhood I had readily and completely embraced the self-image of "high achiever." I excelled at sports, grades were easy if I applied myself, and the accolades from adults for my intellect and maturity filled me up. I started my first business out of my parents' garage at 15 and used the money to pursue cycling. I had some success and turned pro at age 21. By anyone's standards I was a poster child for a disciplined and driven person. But while it appeared that way, I'd given little thought to exactly where I wanted to go. I was churning and burning—so busy *doing* that I rarely, if ever, took time to just *be*. I was superman, or so I thought. I not only didn't smell the roses—I blew the petals off them as I raced by. It was fun, but I was reaching exhaustion. As husband and father who did everything, fixed everything, and tried to play superman, I'd recently reached an acute point of frustration and bitterness as I ran from one task to another, thinking, *I just can't withstand this.* It was honestly the first time I'd even entertained the thought. Not that I'd never met a limit, but I'd never honestly admitted it or conceived that anything was truly an actual limit.

What dawned on me as I thought through the 150 (now near 250!) guests I'd had deep discussions with on my podcast, was that they were of course very driven. Like me. But they were much clearer on exactly where they were going. And why. They had achievements. So did I. But they also had boundaries: they understood they weren't superhuman, and in that self-awareness and compassion they had peace. I was sorely missing the boundaries and peace. How had I been so blind, pursuing achievements but not stopping long enough to really consider what I wanted to achieve and why, and not realizing that trying to be limitless is not an achievement, but a myth?

That morning, I wrote, just a couple of pages at first. The holidays were approaching and I told my kids the only gift I wanted was for them to follow along through the main categories of life fulfillment and consider what they truly valued and wanted and write it down. I did a rare solo podcast on the topic, soon following with a part two. In podcasting we often get reviews on the overall show, but seldom on specific podcasts. These episodes, however, received a good number of reviews and even personal messages. It felt too big to just leave at that.

I'd created some audiences before and was actively blogging and podcasting and twice came to the table with literary agents to pursue a book. As much as I adore writing, I just hadn't found the motive to slow down enough to devote to a book. Here though, I found it—thanks to a motivation born out of personal gratitude (for values and healthy drive I was aware of) and pain (from missing values and errant drive I was unaware of). I had a sizable podcast and audience at this point in the self-help category, and when I realized what I most desired for my kids was for them to consider and be clear on what they really valued and wanted in life, I knew I'd found reason enough to write a book.

TWO MYTHS I DISPEL IN THIS BOOK

The first myth is, some people are driven and some are not. One thing I've long been aware of is that everyone has drive. I define *drive* as "a very strong energy and determination to achieve a goal or satisfy a need." It applies equally to a struggling student, a billionaire, someone trying to buy their first home, or a top politician. *Everyone*, and I mean everyone, has a very strong energy and determination to achieve a goal or satisfy a need. We are all driven. Some just want to get to less productive destinations than others.

Myth number two is that being driven alone equals being happy, fulfilled, and at peace. We applaud and glorify high performance and achievement, but we seldom give attention to whether the high-achieving person is actually happy. Or fulfilled. Or at peace. Personally, I had a lot of fulfillment and a decent amount of happiness, but not so much peace from all the drive. True success is having drive and knowing where and why you're driving and doing so with joy and grace.

THE SOLUTION FOR YOU

With those myths in mind, it's now clear that you have all the drive you need within you. But that doesn't mean you've been using your drive to move you in a beneficial or the right direction and with the right mindset. To get your drive focused and directed is more a matter of awareness than pure motivation.

As we walk through the key areas of life fulfillment and reveal what you value, you'll find the needed awareness and understand what drives you. You'll find all the capacity within you, and you'll be going in the direction needed to achieve what is important to you.

PART ONE

DRIVING SCHOOL

CHAPTER 1

Being Driven Is Just a Thought Away

At age 19, Ben Hardy was the embodiment of everything I most feared for my own children and the younger generation, and yet 15 years later he was a guest on my podcast for the third time with yet another bestselling book. What flipped the switch from his purposeless and hopeless life to one of infinite promise and high-performance drive is one of the most unexpected stories I've ever encountered. That makes him a perfect muse to help us understand why we are completely wrong about how we perceive so-called "driven" people and how we can trigger our own drive to accomplish what we care about in life.

Ben was the oldest of three boys who grew up in a religious home. The family's foundation was built on faith, with clear guideposts for how to live one's life. This made it all the more shocking when Ben's world blew up, at the tender age of 11, when his parents went through a brutal divorce. His mom and dad walked away entirely from the religious structure that had been the primary tenet of their existence. He recalls, "My parents then became completely different people than I thought they were." While his mom threw herself into a struggling health club business, his dad fell into a depression and soon became addicted to meth.

Ben's father declined rapidly, his house becoming a toxic environment for a preteen boy. Ben says, "We'd be in one room playing video games and in the next room were these weird drug addicts, and my friends would be asking what the heck was going on. But it just became the new normal." Meanwhile Ben's mom was putting in 80-hour weeks at the health club and was rarely around.

With Ben's parents living just a few miles from each other, he bounced back and forth between their homes, but he spent the majority of his time in a meaningless distraction of video games. "I graduated from high school but not even sure how, as I missed so many days," he recalls. "I had no stability, no job, no work ethic, and no future in mind. I basically existed in a trauma state."

As his father's home became more dangerous, Ben found himself couch surfing at a cousin's house and spending up to 15 hours a day playing *World of Warcraft*. To any outside observer, Ben had little to no hope for anything positive to come from his life. Yet slowly and steadily, he became aware of the crumbling and vacant lives of those around him, and the idea began growing in his mind that if he didn't do something different, he would end up succumbing to his surroundings and fade into oblivion.

So he decided to do something, anything, to change. No big event happened. No climactic circumstance arose. Just a small, dawning realization. This is how drive is triggered for the majority of people. It's rarely a fancy, tragic, or fairytale event. Too many people wait for some big event to happen to them and never see the dawn. So we must let go of the myth that some people are driven and some are not, when in fact it's more a matter of some people discovering a reason to be driven and some not discovering one.

You must also understand that being driven is not all or nothing. It is possible you can have great drive and success in one area of your life where you have clear and authentic motives yet encounter failure in other areas of your life where your motives are unclear, unhealthy, and possibly hidden, and you find your drive taking you in unfulfilling directions. This is massively frustrating and yet far too normal. We want success to beget success, but how often do you witness people who realize great success in one area of their lives and massive failings in other areas? This has actually become an accepted part of success in our performance-oriented culture. It's OK to have three failed marriages if you are worth millions. It's OK to be a bestselling, Pulitzer Prize–winning author and be physically or psychologically wrecked at a relatively young age. As if we expect that with any great success and gain in one area of our lives we must also endure an equally great sacrifice and loss in another area. We get to viewing our life as a zero-sum game with a winning side and a losing side. This errant view drives many people to just stay in the mediocre middle, afraid of great failure or success, and thinking they must coincide. Do you really want to accept this for your life? Again, this "big high/big low" story line makes great movies, but it is not the norm. I assure you that you can have great drive in *all* areas of your life and achieve fulfillment across the board. That's why I wrote this book.

Regarding Ben's story, I could say the rest is history. But let's take a closer look at the unassuming trajectory that quickly transformed video-gaming, aimless Ben into Benjamin Hardy, PhD, top blogger and multi-bestselling author.

As Ben's nuclear family imploded, he was able to retain two positive influences in his life: his grandfather and a former pastor from his church who made the effort to stay in touch with him. He told me these men were the small lights in his life who sparked the hope of there being a better life for him. Right after his twentieth birthday, a time when Ben was, in his words, "distracted from reality," he left for a church mission that would become for him a turning point for a better life. "I believed in God," said Ben, "but initially I signed up for selfish reasons, hoping it would just lead to better opportunities for my life." Ben's younger brother had struggled with addiction since the divorce and continues to this day. His other brother is autistic and continues living at home with their parents. But in the mission, Ben found purpose, a significant interest in personal growth, and a knack for writing.

Almost overnight, Ben went from playing video games all day to walking the streets and evangelizing to people. Over the next two years he studied spirituality and personal development, particularly the work of Stephen Covey, and fervently journaled his thoughts and beliefs. "On average I journaled for an hour a day and at this point probably have 50 or 60 fully filled-out journals," says Ben. Importantly, while Ben was serving his church mission, his father turned away from his addiction, got clean, and even got involved in addiction recovery support through his church.

Ben developed a love for learning and writing and made the firm decision that this was the direction he wanted to pursue for his life. He got a college degree, earning straight As, and graduated in three years, ultimately getting his PhD in organizational psychology four years later. His prolific reading and journaling helped him develop his knack for writing, which he put to use on the Medium blog platform, where he quickly amassed a following and became their number one writer. He converted that following into an email list of over 150,000 fans, which earned him a six-figure advance for his first book, *Willpower Doesn't Work*. He's since written four other bestselling books. Most excitingly, he married his dream girl, and they are raising their six kids in Orlando, Florida.

Ben doesn't dwell much on his personal story of transformation these days, and I would have missed it if he hadn't briefly mentioned being 19 and playing video games all day in a podcast episode I did with him about one of his books. He initially played it down when I asked him to give me the full story. We all tend to minimize our stories and miss how profound they can be.

Ben's story is a great example of the innocuous dawning that triggers most driven people.

YOU HAVE ALL THE DRIVE YOU NEED

Not only are we held back by the crippling myth that some people are driven and some are not, but we also erroneously believe we must have some massive event to cause us to rise from the ashes. In fact, this concept is sold to us continually in most stories and movies we consume. It makes for a great story but waiting for the big event rarely makes for a great life, as it seldom happens to us. We need to happen to it. And we can. We have all the ingredients, but we often get the recipe wrong. We can fix that.

To reveal how attached we are to the idea of waiting for something to happen to us to finally pour gas on our drive, I point to one of my favorite authors, Donald Miller. In his book *A Million Miles in a Thousand Years*, he says, "A story is a character who wants something and overcomes conflict to get it." This is what most epic movies are made of: A normal guy or gal is ambling along and has what Don says is "an inciting incident." The person responds in dramatic fashion and turns from "zero to hero." But this concept often leaves us looking and waiting for a radical or supernatural inciting incident of our own, something to happen so we can have a big transformation. Yet this is not how the average person becomes driven. The average story is like Ben's.

Drive comes from a realization. A dawning. And then a decision. No watershed moment. No tragic event. Nobody pushing or pulling us. It might not make for a climactic, exciting movie, but it can offer hope that being driven is just a thought and a decision away. In Ben's case, Act 1 is where he's wasting away his life on video games all day with no personal development of his own. But in Act 2 he's accepting yet another big advance for sharing his personal development wisdom with all of us. Let's look again at what took Ben from aimless and unmotivated one day to Mr. Driven the next:

1. Ben became aware of what he did and did not want.
2. Ben was in agreement with his motives.
3. Ben had an incentive from the consequences of staying or going.

He discovered what he wanted, or just as powerful, what he did *not* want, and why. He saw the failing people around him and realized he did not want to end up like them. And the only way to change things was to change things. Do something different. He looked at his options, saw only one, and took it. Super simple. And what followed was an efficient life transformation.

I just covered a very important point and a key aspect of motivation that is often missed. We are generally implored to focus on what we desire. Yet behavioral psychology teaches us that humans are far more motivated by pain than by desire. So Ben's awareness of what he *did not want* is significant. As you consider what you want and why, you may find more traction and motive in considering what you *don't* want. We generally think of the risk of doing something and fail to consider the risk of *not* doing something. "If I quit this job I hate, my income may suffer, my spouse may get scared, and I may have to miss a few episodes of my favorite show while job hunting or starting a side business." Right. And on the other side, "Yet if I don't quit this job, I hate I may get an ulcer, have a panic attack, and ultimately get fired anyway as it's hard to be competent when you hate what you do." Desire or pain. Figure out what motivates you and use it.

I admit, after hearing Ben's story, I started to question some of my parenting techniques, as a father who is striving to teach my kids the value of a work ethic and personal relationship skills, and to ultimately graduate from Harvard and/or start a million-dollar business before age 20. I can expose them to ideas and opportunities to help prepare them for a successful life, but first, there is no guarantee, and second, do I know what success will feel like to them? Ben had been given absolutely no guidance from his parents, but he found drive on his own and figured the rest out. I'm not minimizing my efforts to equip my kids, but Ben's story has inspired me to focus more on the bigger-picture issues of faith and purpose and relational health that will more likely instill my children with a motive to be driven toward something of value. Anything. As it stands now, none of my kids have graduated from Harvard or started a million-dollar business. They are, however, great, caring humans I'm so proud of.

But don't miss the powerful truth about motive, which circles back to Donald Miller's quip about a good story. It's a character who wants something and overcomes conflict to get it. You won't really value your accomplishments in life unless you have some sort of struggle. Expecting resistance isn't being pessimistic: rather, it's building up your ability to succeed. If I gifted you with an all-expense-paid trip to your favorite vacation spot but said the airline would have a problem and you'd be stranded midway for a couple of days, you'd say, "Fine!" and probably make plans to enjoy the time. But without the forewarning, anytime you spoke of the otherwise glorious trip you'd likely dwell on the "horrible delay." Expect the conflict you find on your way toward your goals, and when it inevitably comes you can recognize it as a sign you're doing something worthwhile. Don't let it discourage you.

THERE IS NO NEUTRAL

If you are waiting for the stars to align or simply hoping for something to happen to you to trigger your drive, I'm now freeing you from the wait. It will likely never come. Or if it does, you'll be less able to capitalize on it. To go back to a previous example, this happens every day to people in jobs they don't like but won't leave. But if while they were working the current job, they took a second job called "Go find a better job," they would come up with a best-case solution. They'd have time to do the research and find a job that really fits them, meanwhile still getting paid from the old job, and have a perfect transition. A new, wonderful job, and never miss a day's pay. Instead, the vast majority of folks just hold on to the dreaded job until they get laid off, which, may I point out, sometimes happens to people who don't like what they do or where they work. Then comes the mad scramble to find something to make ends meet. If they do find a better job somewhere else, they're likely to say getting fired is the best thing that happened to them. But chances are they still settle for less than what is possible, as time doesn't allow them to do a thorough search and secure a better job without some time in between with no pay.

This is what happens when we wait for the "inciting incident" to give us motive and make us the driven people we always wanted to be. It either never comes or when it does, we're often unprepared. Ben was lucky that he found his awareness at age 19, but many don't find it until far later in life, if at all. Two interesting things to note about happy, fulfilled, and successful people: one, they can generally tell you when and what it was that gave them their motive to be driven, and two, I've not yet found one who said they wish they'd found it later. Most of us have significant regret for the time we spent languishing.

We are ultimately talking about being *proactive* instead of *reactive*. Elementary, I'll grant you, but dramatically profound and rare. We are a reactive culture, and we even reward the concept. An easy-to-understand analogy is healthcare and doctors. My great friend and frequent podcast cohost Randy James is a medical doctor. He put in his time fixing what was broken in his patients but was ultimately drawn to an interest in prevention. Today he is an expert in Functional Medicine, which endeavors to *prevent* illness and disease instead of merely treating and managing it as Western medicine is built to do. If a patient comes to him with high blood pressure, Randy's quest is to find what is causing the high blood pressure and correct it instead of just prescribing a medication to artificially manage the issue.

It's the concept of "upstream versus downstream," illustrated by the story of a guy who sees a person struggling in the current of a strong river and jumps in to save that person. Moments later he sees another person in the same plight, and he saves that one too. The first instinct might be to throw life jackets to the swimmers or get a net to try to catch them as they go downstream. That's the general mindset of traditional medicine. But as the story continues in this case, after scores of people are saved, the man gets a bigger idea. How about walking upstream to figure out why so many people are falling in to begin with? Brilliant! So instead of waiting for something to happen to you and trigger more drive and trying to motivate and inspire yourself, let's get into the root issue of why your drive is lacking or not producing the intended results.

Habits has become a key buzzword in the self-help world, and rightfully so. Regardless of anything we say or think, we are simply the sum of our daily habits. My favorite theologian, Frederick Buechner, wisely said, "If you want to know who you are, watch your feet. Because where your feet take you, that is who you are." I've greatly benefited from the research and influence of Charles Duhigg (*The Power of Habit*) and James Clear (*Atomic Habits*). Yet we generally miss the notion that adopting good habits assumes one already has a clear motive in the first place and is thus driven enough to act on those habits. Showcasing good habit methodologies to an unmotivated person with no drive is akin to getting your teenager excited to do household chores. It's pointless—they just don't care. Bribe, cajole, threaten, you name it, but you're pissing in the wind. The only thing that will work long term is to realize a paradigm shift. Like your teenager going to serve in a developing country and coming back with a realization of their privilege and deciding for themselves they want to be a responsible and contributing person who likes to do chores. We need a reason we authentically agree with for ourselves.

There are few if any greater benefits to your life than getting clear on what you want and why you want it, which in itself creates drive. One of Zig Ziglar's many famous quotes is, "There is no such thing as a lazy person; [they are] either sick or uninspired." If you find yourself uninspired in life, or in any one area of your life, you can build inspiration. You can create drive.

HOW TO DRIVE TO THE CORRECT DESTINATION

Up to this point, I've defined *drive* as something that you already have within you, and it's either turned on or not. This is not entirely accurate, as very few perspectives on human behavior are absolutely black and white. After all, we are complex creatures. Let's flip the script on Ben Hardy going from being not driven to driven. In reality this is not true. He was always driven. But sometimes we drive blindly and end up at destinations we do not desire.

When we talk about having drive and being driven, we naturally envision someone striving fervently toward positive and worthy goals and outcomes. A driven person is a valiant person, right? If you're driven to become a celebrity, pro athlete, or C-suite executive, or to help people in a developing country, we applaud you. But if you're driven to addiction or crime, we don't always recognize your drive. But either way, whether it's used for good or ill, drive it is. Think back to Ben's meth-addicted father. Meth addicts would probably top the list of the "Driven Hall of Fame" if it existed. Addicts are acutely aware of what they want and why and will literally kill for it. How about gang members and career criminals? Even Ben himself playing video games for 15 hours a day. Was this not drive? The drive to escape the hurt, insecurity, and lack of control he felt in his life? In the world of video games, he could take action and overcome and voyeuristically feel the progress we long for as humans. This is a key issue in our culture today: why people are driven to virtual environments and activities. If we don't fulfill our core desires in the real world, we'll manufacture them artificially. Even a counterfeit is better than nothing. But we have drive in us, and we must exert it somewhere, even if it's binging Netflix on the couch, connecting to characters on a screen who are driven to do something.

Imagine twins who live together. One wakes at 5 a.m. to meditate, exercise, and plan their day. This twin is showered and out the door by 7:30 a.m. to put in a solid day of inspiring work, meet with friends and colleagues, have dinner with a romantic interest, and then home to read and write by candlelight before some breathing exercises and lights out at 9 p.m. The other twin sleeps in till 10 a.m. Or sometimes 2 p.m. Crawls out of bed to scroll social media for an hour (or three) while munching on Cap'n Crunch and drinking bad coffee. Pulls up DoorDash to deliver a box of fried chicken and fries; then on to some serious TV viewing until 2 or 3 a.m. Which twin is driven? They both are, and they are both feeding appetites leading to certain outcomes.

As a kid I was fascinated by books from *Ripley's Believe It or Not* and *The Guinness Book of World Records*. I'll always remember the story and pictures of Jon Brower Minnoch, who weighed in at 1,400 pounds and is still listed as the heaviest man of all time. When we hear a story like this, we find ourselves asking, "What would drive someone to do such a thing?"

It takes an enormous amount of drive. Often the drive to do something harmful and detrimental exceeds the drive to do something positive. We all have drive, and lots of it. The key is getting it going in the directions we desire. When we know what we want and why, and have an authentic drive, we drive toward life-enriching goals and objectives. When we are unclear on what we want and why, we will still be driven, but we won't end up where we truly want to go.

Rally car racing is a two-person sport. The driving is generally off-road on uneven terrain, and blind corners are the norm, not the exception. To drive at the highest speed requires precise planning, so drivers will pre-drive the course, and the co-driver will record it in their pace notes. The reality is, visual driving is not fast enough. If drivers relied only on what they see on the course, the time would be far slower than having a co-driver studying the course and taking notes and telling them not just what is coming, but what to do, such as which gear to be in, or whether they need to go right or left over a hump in the road, after a blind corner, or at the next intersection. The driver is driving, but they take direction from the co-driver, who has the power to take them the right way (or the wrong way) or lead them into a win (or an imminent crash).

In your life you are never, ever driving solo. It's impossible. If I take a blank robot and load it with one solitary program to drive a country road, it just does it. End of story. You, however, happen to be a human. When you drive such a country road, especially at high speed, you are joined by many copilots best known as *motives*. We often refer to them as the voices in our head. Our thoughts. Some we are aware of, but many we are not. And they copilot us to the right or wrong destinations. If you're 30 years old, you have 30 years of exposure and programming affecting your emotions on your drive. You could be ecstatic about this country drive, or absolutely terrified. And this massively affects how fast or slow you go, how bumpy the ride is or isn't, the radio volume, temperature, and ultimately the direction you go and destination you arrive at.

You have some areas of your life where you know your co-driving motives and you're getting the fulfilling results you want. Awesome. This is the goal for all areas of your life. Then there are those other areas where you have a co-driving motive you are not in agreement with: the places where you experience frustration, guilt, anger, and even despair. In extreme cases, a co-driving motive has grabbed you, slammed you over into the passenger's seat, and taken hold of the steering wheel, and you are not at all in control.

The good news is you can ensure your motives are driving you the right direction—the right direction for *you*. You can take control even among the dire programming of trauma, tragedy, and fear. Being in full control as the driver doesn't mean you must overcome everything coming from your co-driving motives, but you can learn to be aware, manage them, and course correct.

I find a very good analogy for creating drive and how we view driven people in the world's fascination with comic book superheroes.

Bruce Banner was accidentally exposed to gamma radiation while testing a bomb, which gave him superhuman size and strength, and he became the Hulk. Jessica Campbell accidentally got doused in toxic chemicals in a car crash and gained superhuman strength and the ability to fly, becoming Jessica Jones. Peter Parker was bitten by a radioactive spider, which gave him the speed and strength of a spider, the ability to stick to surfaces, and a "Spider-Sense" warning him of immediate danger: Spider-Man. These people had something happen to them through no fault or credit to themselves.

On the other hand, Tony Stark didn't wait around for an accident to happen to him. Instead, he engineered his own superpowers to become Iron Man, arguably the primary hero of the entire Marvel Avengers series. What is also significant is that once he built one Iron Man exoskeleton, he could duplicate it infinitely.

We must stop viewing drive and driven people as accidentally or luckily falling into this great power while everyone else is sitting around with the short end of the stick or hoping something significant will happen to them and they'll miraculously become driven. The reality is that many healthfully driven people simply manufactured their drive like Tony Stark and are living Iron Man lives today. Nobody needs to wait for drive to happen to them. Let's go build your drive.

MOST HAPPINESS COMES FROM THE DRIVE ITSELF

Most people will likely pick up this book because they are eager to bolster their drive to achieve desired results and solve problems in their lives, and rightly so. Yet this doesn't consider what I've found to be the greatest benefit and payoff, which is simply waking up each morning with hope and excitement for making progress. That enthusiasm is the antidote for so much of the apathy, depression, and despair people are experiencing.

In my early podcasting days, I came across a guy named Joshua Spodek, a professor at NYU who works as an astrophysicist and author. Two things about Joshua caught my attention: one, he had become known for doing sets of burpees for over 3,000 days in a row, and two, he had written a blog titled *SIDCHA*, an acronym for "self-imposed daily challenging healthy activities." I had him on my show to talk about this, and what he revealed was revelatory to me.

Josh found that SIDCHA's big payoff was not the result of the activities themselves, but rather the accumulative mental benefit from being someone who does SIDCHAs. The benefit from doing burpees nobody is forcing or rewarding you to do is that you become the type of person who can do hard things when no one is forcing or rewarding you. That is a strength and benefit far greater than anything burpees can give you. I'm naturally a results-oriented guy—I was a pro cyclist. You only get prize money for winning, and you only get street cred for your latest result; there is no status in the sport for the journey itself. So when I first read Josh's article on SIDCHA, I resonated with the end results, or the payoff, you receive from *self-imposed daily challenging healthy activities*. You train every day, and the payoff is, you win bike races. You eat clean every day, and the payoff is wellness. You learn something every day, and the payoff is knowledge. I really don't like burpees, but I like being the kind of mentally strong person who will do them.

We know far too many stories of people who were driven to achieve a result and found despair as well. They were focused on the payoff and not enjoying the drive. When you realize the benefit from finding that your drive is not simply to achieve a desired result or solve a problem, but to become a more joyful and fulfilled person who looks forward to each and every day, you will find a consistent, joyful drive that never leaves you.

CHAPTER SUMMARY

▶ Drive is just a thought away. Don't wait for something big to happen. Don't wait for anything to happen. Most drive and driven people are simply a result of basic awareness—being aware of what is happening and gaining clarity on what you want to happen and veering that direction.

▶ Drive is often segmented. You will often find that you are adequately driven and achieving success in some areas of your life, and feel you are making similar efforts in other areas of life but lacking the results you desire. You are likely being driven by something deeper you are not aware of that conflicts with your true desires. You will find chapters in this book on each core area of life where you can dig in to the lacking area to get clarity on what is driving you and discern what you really want to be driving you.

▶ Sustaining drive doesn't come from massive effort, grit, and willpower, but simply a course change. If you're driving from the hills of Tennessee to the beaches of Florida and realize you want to go to the mountains of Colorado, just turn right. You may need a little reorienting as you envision the environment of the mountains instead of the beach, but don't be misled that it takes a monumental buildup of effort.

▶ You have all the drive you need. Keep reminding yourself of this. Nobody is more driven than you—some just have more clear direction on where they want to go.

▶ Awareness, agreement, and incentive are the key to your healthy and true drive. These are what you will map out in this book in each of the seven key areas of life fulfillment.

▶ What you don't want may help give you clarity if you are struggling with what you do want.

▶ What you want should be a struggle. If it has true value and fulfillment, it will duly inspire and challenge you.

▶ Drive alone is not the key. You must have the right destination in mind. And the right destination is up to you.

▶ Enjoy the drive. It is often where the most fulfillment comes from, eclipsing the destination itself.

CHAPTER 2

Unlocking Your Unique Drive

Twenty-eight-year-old Alexander Selkirk was in essence a legalized pirate for the British Crown and a known hot-head. In October 1704, while serving as a navigator on the *Cinque Ports* and anchored 418 miles west of Valparaiso, Chile, he demanded to be left on the nearest large island, in rebellion to his captain who he felt was overly arrogant. The captain agreed, and Alexander got off the ship. He had expected some of his shipmates to join him, as many shared his sentiments, but when to his dismay he realized they would not, he asked to reboard and was denied.

He remained alone on the island for four years and four months.

As later documented by Alexander's descendant Bruce Selcraig for the *Smithsonian* magazine, upon disembarking the ship Alexander was given "bedding, a musket, pistol, gunpowder, hatchet, knife, his navigation tools, a pot for boiling food, two pounds of tobacco, some cheese and jam, a flask of rum and his Bible."[1] After an initial time of despondency, he learned where to harvest food, how to avoid predators, where to find shelter, and how to pass the time and maintain his sanity.

On a fateful day in February 1709 he spied a ship named the *Duke* and was rescued. The *Duke*'s captain, Woodes Rogers, was so taken with Alexander's story that he and Richard Steele wrote an account of it in 1712, which provided Alexander with relative fame. They cited how the island transformed Alexander from his prior delinquent condition, and as Steele wrote, "his Life [became] one continual Feast, and his Being much more joyful than it had before been irksome." They wrote about Alexander learning to live without his vices and indulgences of alcohol, tobacco, and even salt, and how he became so nimble running barefoot on the rocky hills he could chase down any goat he wanted. He spent much time singing hymns and praying and relishing the solitude.

British author Daniel Defoe published the story in 1719 as *The Life and Strange Surprizing Adventures of Robinson Crusoe*. An initial printing of 1,000 copies quickly went to a fourth printing, and the name of Crusoe became wildly famous. The novel inspired later castaway stories like *The Swiss Family Robinson* and many others, thereby turning a disaster into a tale of not only survival but flourishing.

We now have untold books, movies, and more containing similar lessons of finding oneself with limited resources and a requirement to sustain life with what you have. In 1985, when I was 14 years old, the TV series *MacGyver* began and ran for seven years. I rarely missed an episode. I was greatly inspired by the character, a secret agent known for his genius-level intellect, refusal to use guns, and a profound engineering ability that enabled him to make do with nearly any available resource to fight off the enemy and save the world. Today we even refer to masterful making-do as "MacGyvering." From Crusoe to MacGyver, these characters illustrate what we already know to be true: limited resources spark the drive to not just survive, but thrive. Put another way, the old adage holds up: "Necessity *is* the mother of invention."

When faced with infinite resources, we fall into confusion, frustration, and apathy. It's too overwhelming. A well-known example is the story of two psychologists, Sheena Iyengar and Mark Leeper, who studied jam sales at a local market. When 24 varieties were offered, more people took interest, yet when only 6 options existed people were 10 times more likely to actually purchase jam.[2] Think of how you feel at a restaurant when the menu has six pages and 100 options. It's overwhelming. This is incredibly important in business—whether you are a business owner or not. Giving others too many options can hurt your chances of getting the results or answers you're looking for.

When faced with finite supplies and options, people often find inspiration and hope. When we have endless options, there is great pressure to create perfection, which leads us to feeling overwhelmed and impotent. Yet with limits, we come to believe in possibility. What's more, when we discover our unique traits that we can draw from to construct and direct our drive, that's when the pedal really hits the metal.

YOU CAN'T BE ANYTHING YOU WANT, BUT YOU CAN BE GREAT

When you tell someone they can be and do anything, you are crippling them, as it offers up too many options. Not to mention, it's a flat-out lie. Even if it were true that you could do and be anything, you couldn't be and do some things very well. And while we romanticize being an exception to the rule, we seldom want to plan for it. Instead of our abilities being limitless, we are all uniquely gifted with propensities that allow us to find our drive and ensure success in a manner truly fitting to our individual nature.

The average height of an NBA player is 6'4.7" and weight is 217 pounds. But back in 1987 everyone learned the name of Muggsy Bogues, who was drafted twelfth overall by the Washington Bullets. He was an exceptional player, but the reason we know him is because he stood at 5'3" and weighed in at only 136 pounds. But check this out: the average vertical leap of today's 6'4" NBA player is 28 inches, while Muggsy's was a startling 44 inches. Incredible. Impressive. Muggsy gives us all hope to overcome the odds against us. But the odds of NBA stardom are far greater if you're big and tall. All of us have our greatest opportunity for success well within our ability and capacity. We just need to put together our drive from the ingredients we all have.

In keeping with the *drive* theme, let's talk about cars and equate you to an automobile of some type. You're on your own island of life like Alexander, or you find yourself like MacGyver, assessing what you can do with what you have. And some will have it easier than others. Again, take hope in Muggsy, and if you find yourself with difficult parts, you can still be a champion. But I'm not minimizing the reality of your life and hardship. I'm offering true hope and possibility, but not sugarcoating it. You may need to work harder and jump twice as high as everyone else for the same slam dunk.

Visualize yourself as a car. There is a frame. An engine. A body. Wheels and brakes and so forth. Some of you may envision your car as the Volkswagen Thing that looked like a kindergartener's crayon depiction of a car-truck combo. You may think of yourself as an efficient electric Prius. Or a gas-guzzling Humvee. The point is, we all have the same general framework, though often vastly different styles of components. Some of your components you chose, some you didn't. Some you can choose, some you can't. There is vast opportunity for upgrades and redesigns, but the possibilities are not endless. Which is good news.

Many of you will find you have been driving toward things unfitting for you. They might fit an expectation somewhere, or a misaligned desire, and it's driving you toward repeated frustration and burnout and you don't understand why. Few people will find themselves feeling limited by what I'm about to reveal, and most will find new freedoms. More realistic and reasonable freedoms. Let's go.

THE FIVE GEARS OF DRIVE

A word of caution and hope before we dive in here. What I propose next can initially feel harsh if you've had a difficult upbringing and/or trauma in your past. I don't minimize this, but instead, honor it. The majority of the nearly 200 successful, happy, high-achieving guests I've had on my podcasts have shared significant difficulties and traumas. They are the ones who were courageous and strove not to be limited, but empowered by what happened to them. I have faith you are like them too.

In Part Two of this book we'll look at what inherently influences you in your key areas of life fulfillment regarding each of the five gears, but following is a "CliffsNotes" explanation.

First Gear: What Is Inherent
The issue of nature versus nurture is a highly debated topic, but in the world of self-help and personal development, we

weigh heavily on the side of nurture. And rightly so. What you can't change about yourself, you can't change. So why spend much time dwelling on it? Focus on what you *can* change.

Sonja Lyubomirsky is a professor of psychology at UC Riverside and a leading expert on happiness. She is credited with the widely utilized Happiness Pie Chart, which is headlined "What Determines Happiness" and shows that 50 percent of happiness is from genetic set points, 40 percent from intentional activity, and 10 percent circumstances.[3] When I first came upon this, thanks to podcast guest Niyc Pidgeon, I was somewhat disappointed in the high percentage of the genetic set point. But in researching further I found that many of her peers struggled not with the stats, but the perception of genes *determining* happiness, as opposed to being just what they say, set points. Meaning your genetics are not 50 percent responsible for how happy you can be, but statistically they will have 50 percent influence on where your happiness starts. Thus, you can be the absolute happiest person on the planet, even if all your ancestors were a combo of Eeyore and Ebenezer Scrooge. You just may have a longer gap to make up than if you came from a heritage of Pollyannas. This is a very relevant way to look at your possible genetic predispositions. One, just because you had sad people behind you doesn't mean you necessarily have their sad genetics in you. Although you might. But even so, it's simply a possible emotional starting point, and regarding the key areas of life that matter for your overall joy and fulfillment, you need to consider more than just genetic predispositions. You can focus on things you *can* change. We're not concerned here with traits you can't change like curly hair, cleft chin, or dimples.

The day you were born you had some genetic drive *propensities* already built into you, and gaining awareness of them now gets you up and running, or shifts you into "first gear." I like to think of these propensities like a CD, the cool disc that replaced the cassette tape in my youth. Back then we would save digital files on a CD, which seems antiquated now. When you saved a small amount of files, you could actually tilt the CD in the right light and see where the grooves had been etched in.

Those etches are like your genetics—what was "saved" on your drive before your skin ever hit the air of Earth. In faith-based cultures, credence is given to "the sins of the fathers" being passed down three or four generations, and science as well has made the case that what happened to your great-great-great-great-grandparents could still exist in your DNA.

But why would that matter? The point is not whether your genetic makeup is helping or hurting, as again, it's well proven that many people with the worst things in their past can succeed at the highest levels. Those initial grooves can never be totally undone. They can, however, be recognized and managed. I simply want you aware of what you've got to work with so you can better leverage and/or mitigate what you find.

If you came from a long line of people who pursued learning and growth and had many successes and achievements in their lives, your set point may be higher. Conversely your family may have come from a culture ravaged by war and tragedy, who were crippled in fear. You may have grown up with the idea that it's best to lie low and not rock the boat. In either case, your heritage wouldn't dictate your capacity for drive, but it can help you understand why being driven comes more naturally or is a bit more of a challenge. Knowing as much as you can simply helps you prepare accordingly.

A word of encouragement to those who feel their drive may be hampered by something they can't put their finger on. Generally, I'm not a fan of victim mentality. In this case, however, I offer it up in an effort to help you find grace for yourself. Maybe you have a genetic disposition that might make it more difficult to assemble your drive. Consider accepting this and allowing yourself to have some peace about it. It is what it is. Then, go about assembling your drive anyway. Like Muggsy Bogues, you will need to put in extra work to increase your vertical jump, per se. Your capacity is not limited, just more challenged. You are up for it.

Second Gear: What You've Been Exposed To

The concept of brainwashing came to prominence in the 1950s during the Korean War. Journalist Edward Hunter penned a headline in the *Miami Daily News* stating, "Brain-washing Tactics Force Chinese into Ranks of Communist Party."[4] It was apparently the best way America had to explain why anyone would be communist, and they depicted the Chinese as some mix of robot-zombies. The issue escalated when a large number of American prisoners of war falsely confessed war crimes, petitioned the US government to end the war, and even signed confessions of crimes they had not committed.

What followed was much research on POWs and brainwashing and ultimately the psychiatric study of mind control. One psychiatrist pinpointed some key aspects of wartime brainwashing I find to be profoundly comparable to, of all things, growing up under the influence of a parent— which, to some degree, we've all had experience with.

Two primary aspects of brainwashing occur when you are in an environment where someone else has complete control and forces you to confess things you do not believe to be true. Unless you've ever done some serious therapy, and the right kind, you have accepted life as you see it, and you see it in the way you were allowed to. It can be daunting to realize that in our formative years, we were under the power of the same primary tenants of wartime brainwashing and mind control.

I'll own this in regard to my own family.

My kids did not choose to be born, as they will occasionally remind me when I'm trying to convince them of something. Nor did they choose to grow up at 9,300 feet above sea level in a national forest in a big, weird house with walls built out of straw bales. This alone dictated much of their "reality," as they don't know what living in a neighborhood with neighbors is like. For most of their upbringing we didn't have cell service at the house, which qualifies as teenage torture. For many years they were homeschooled, and some of them have some disappointment with this. We limited TV or extracurricular activities with the older kids out of good intentions, but some of them ended up feeling isolated. They didn't choose what we bought from the grocery and cooked for them, and so on.

Greater than these circumstantial realities were the morals, values, and general life perspectives we bestowed upon them. Of course I think my view on life is righteous and good, but it is just my individual view. As open-minded as we want to be, unless we just neglect our children (another form of brainwashing), we have to advocate some views on living, and we did.

You get the picture. As a parent or authority in a child's life, it's impossible not to massively influence them. And you were massively influenced. Again, you have a lot more grooves now etched into the CD of your life. Grooves I don't believe you can fully erase. Grooves of songs repeated to you every day of your entire upbringing. Songs you didn't choose to dance to, but you did. You didn't know any better. Our life's yearning is to trust and belong. Some of our parents or caregivers strove to give us great music to dance to in ways that would lift us up. Others had really hurtful and harmful songs tearing them down.

So what do you do about it? You can create new grooves, as the good news is your CD of life is infinite. Create as many new grooves as you want. Quit listening to the old music. Burn in new songs, and over time, just like with a music playlist on Spotify, you end up not even listening to the old songs.

Regarding your drive and propensity to be driven: Your parents and caregivers gave you your greatest example and a significant set point. You've either followed their lead or rebelled. We see it every day: the parents who glorified and preached being driven, and one kid blindly follows their lead and eventually burns out, while the other blindly rebels and does nothing. Another set of parents constantly tells the kids the world is a bad place and "none of you will amount to anything." One kid accepts it and repeats the pattern and same song, while the other rebels and says, "I'll prove you wrong!" and has wild success yet never achieves a moment's peace or fulfillment.

When we don't know what we authentically want, the vast majority of all our efforts are based on the expectations of our environment and the people around us, and our subsequent acceptance or rejection of those expectations that lacks awareness. This keeps us from creating our own unique reality set apart from our past. The tragedy is, most of us aren't in touch with our authentic wants.

Third Gear: What You Authentically Want

My dad's parents were born Amish. The real deal. Beards, no electricity, and a horse and buggy. They later left the Amish lifestyle but retained its incredibly conservative religion. When my dad was a youth, they actually got a car.

And something was triggered in my dad: a love of cars. He literally built his first car, and I always knew him as the consummate "car guy." I worked along with him in the car business, got subscriptions to *Car & Driver* magazine, and purchased coffee-table books of my favorite European automobiles. I bought my first car at 15, an old, beat-up Porsche 924, and with Dad's help restored it. I even had thoughts of pursuing car racing, but at some point I devoted myself to pro cycling and found myself buying a sensible Subaru wagon to haul bikes and teammates.

From then on, I've treated cars simply as a vessel to get me from point A to B. These days, most of my time is spent driving a 1999 Chevy Suburban and an all-wheel-drive passenger van, hauling kids, bikes, and trash from our mountain home. I finally realized I'm not much of a car guy, but I began as one simply due to my exposure. How errant I would have been if I'd gone into the car business and continued with the exposure of my childhood. I'm grateful my parents advocated exposure to other things and supported me in endeavors they had no experience in. I will admit an abiding penchant for old Euro sports cars, and if I didn't live high up in the Rockies I'd be itching for an old Porsche or Jaguar.

Discerning what we truly want can be disconcerting as we consider how much we haven't even been exposed to. My dad never worked for anyone else his entire life, so all I knew was being an entrepreneur, which I have been my entire life. If he'd been a doctor, there is a good chance I would have followed, just as my buddy Randy did in following his dad's footsteps as a doctor. Would I have liked the military? Farming? High tech? Academia? I don't know; I didn't have any exposure. To determine what you authentically want requires you to understand the influences you've had and open yourself up to new ones.

When Lynne Twist was five years old at a family barbecue, her mom said something so many parents say: that she should "clean her plate because children are starving in Korea." Lynne asked her mother if that was really true, as her mother had actually grown up in Korea, and her mother confirmed that there were children her age in Korea who couldn't eat for days. Lynne says she told herself from that moment on that she would grow up and do something about it.

Fast-forward to age 32, and Lynne attended a seminar led by Werner Erhard, founder of Erhard Seminars Training. Lynne was a mere assistant, taking care of the room and 60 VIP attendees including university professors and renowned music artist John Denver. Werner announced to the group that he was committing himself to ending world hunger and equipping millions of people to help, and temporarily named the initiative The Hunger Project. Lynne found herself in instantaneous tears and struggling to catch her breath, with a deep-rooted feeling that she was supposed to be a part of this project and this was to be her life's work. Lynne spent the next two decades with The Hunger Project, raising millions of dollars, and today she is a recognized global visionary committed to alleviating poverty, ending world hunger, and supporting social justice and environmental sustainability. She has worked with Mother Teresa in Calcutta, in refugee camps in Ethiopia, and in the threatened rain forests of the Amazon.

The good news is you don't have to spend the next year or 10 trying to experience everything on Earth in order to discover what you authentically want. You only need to learn about your natural propensities and predispositions to narrow down the field.

I'm going to prescribe three personality profiles and use myself as an example to show how you can apply them, since

I know me better than anyone else. Our quest is to discern your overall propensities and predispositions. The profiles don't necessarily show proof of your absolute God-given nature, but they do lend telltale signs of the culmination of your genetics and life-wiring.

The DISC and Enneagram are both popular and valuable personality profiles, but I want to throw a relatively new one into the mix from my friend Jonathan Fields at www.sparketype.com. The Sparketype is relatively simple, and Jonathan's focus is to discern what lights you up and drives you in regard to the work you engage in. Mine showcased me as a "Maker" and was valuable to me in confirming I am most inspired and absolutely driven when I am making things. I love a thought or idea and a blank piece of paper to start constructing a framework. I like an idea of a wall, roof, porch, or bunk bed and a pile of wood and screws from which to build a new addition to my home. I like waking to a day totally free to do what I want as it spontaneously comes to mind. This is what lights me up, and the more I cater my life to accommodate it, the more inspired, fulfilled, and driven I am. The test likewise shows what your Anti-Sparketype is to reveal the style that will be most draining. Mine is "Nurture," and my family well knows this about me. It doesn't mean I'm incapable of nurturing, but it's certainly more difficult for me. Let's just say I'm not the most comforting shoulder to cry on. But my kids know to come to me for brainstorming on their next idea and adventure.

The value of these three different personality tests, in tandem with the message of this book, is to help you really zero in on the lifestyle design that you will find most fulfilling to the core of who you really are—that is, your authentic wants. Mix and match them to find threads of truth pointing to your authentic drives. When you do, you'll find a vocational and lifestyle direction that will support your flourishing self.

But you will need to give yourself permission to let go of your programming and the influences you have had, and question if they truly fit you, while also giving yourself freedom to consider new things that may never have crossed your mind before.

I was privileged to grow up in a home that encouraged my Maker propensity, as my parents encouraged me to create and try and risk and fail. They were both consummate entrepreneurs, and making new things out of nothing was the family motto and mission. What a privilege for me. Maybe you've experienced the same, and how wonderful. But imagine if I'd been born into a family where security and precision was most valued? Just like thinking I was into cars, I would likely have just blindly followed suit and tried to fit myself into a mold I'd find forever restricting and uncomfortable. Or I might have rebelled and swung wide into untethered chaos and violent risk.

Fourth Gear: What Motivates You

Brené Brown has become the figurehead for vulnerability and getting in touch with your emotions. She's also one of only a couple of people ever to decline being on my podcast (I hope she reconsiders at some point). But in her book *Atlas of the Heart*, she outlines her extensive research on all the human emotions. I have generally thought of emotions in narrow categories: happy, frustrated, or angry. I had a therapist once who gathered that I was somewhat out of touch with my emotions and gave me a worksheet for my "emotional dashboard" that listed about 15 to help me branch out a bit. Brené lists 87 emotions! But I'm savvy, as Jack Sparrow would say, as I'm appreciating more and more the impact of emotions in all that we do.

We humans, especially those of us who aspire to learn and grow and evolve, believe we make decisions and take action based on logic. Yet the wealth of psychology as well as looking back on my own life prove this to be false—in fact, most of what we do is rooted in emotion. Take most any "unemotional guy" and get him watching a sport he enjoys and tell me he's unemotional. Take the same guy and threaten his family and see how regulated his emotions are. Just because someone controls or is limited in their expression of emotion doesn't mean they don't have them.

What drives you is not logic, it's emotion. Want to be driven? Understand the emotion behind your motives and harness it, so it doesn't harness you. Wherever you are struggling with achieving success in your life, I wager you have a negative emotion sabotaging you. Your logic says one thing, and your emotion says (and does) another. I did this in my finances for a long time. My logic said I wanted to have a successful business and make money, but my emotion was afraid to make money and look like some of the wealthy businessmen I had come to know, who didn't line up with the morality I valued. I was blind to the emotion for so, so long, and even with successful business ventures I sabotaged creating any true wealth.

Hidden motives are the primary saboteur to our desire for drive and success, and this is why we find people having great success and fulfillment in one area of life and failure in another. The effort we put into one endeavor works, but in another, not so much. I refer to it as the *hidden drive*. Going back to my previous analogy of getting you in the driver's seat, often a hidden emotion will hop in there and supplant you. No quantity of self-help or personal development or inspiration will overcome an emotional saboteur.

You've simply got to root out this hidden drive, and a primary focus of this book is to help you do just that.

First, pain and fear are not always bad things when it comes to drive. I really like adrenaline and plummeting down a high-elevation single-track trail on my mountain bike. Fear of the pain of a high-speed impact keeps me in check just enough to avoid major catastrophe—usually. This is a very helpful fear of pain. It was likewise more fear than desire that caused me to build our high mountain home when we didn't have any money, time, or knowledge. I was afraid we wouldn't ever have the dream home till the kids were too old to appreciate it. Again, this was a more fear-based motive I'm OK with. Fear of *not* achieving the goal was stronger than my desire to achieve it. But you want to be aware of your emotions and in agreement with them, thereby putting you in control to harness them appropriately.

Second, we can look at the objective and consider the reality of achieving it and increase the desire—the positive. So many of us have it pretty good, all things considered. Life may never get so painful that it drives us to change, but we still feel a responsibility to continue learning, growing, and evolving. And many have altruistic desires calling them. With greater success, whom could you help and benefit? Or it can be just about the achievement. I've seen many people achieve lifelong ambitions, and the greatest joy was simply how it made them feel about themselves, which is priceless.

You can see how important it is to reveal your emotions and harness them. They are stronger than any logic or justification you will ever come up with.

Fifth Gear: What You Believe In

As the story goes, in 1927 Victor Serebriakoff was 15 when his teacher told him he would never finish school and should drop out and learn a trade. Victor took the advice, and for the next 17 years he wandered around doing a variety of menial jobs. Then when he was 32 years old, Victor took an evaluation that revealed he was a genius with an IQ of 161. Victor went on to write books, secured a number of patents, and became a successful businessman. The kicker came when the former "dunce" was elected president of the International Mensa Society, which has only one membership qualification: an IQ of 140 or more.[5]

We see ourselves based upon what we feel is the proof of our life. The facts. Just as Victor did. He didn't do well in school, an authority figure gave testimony to the obvious facts, and Victor accepted that testimony and acted accordingly. When Victor was later given new proof, he accepted that as well, and subsequently acted accordingly again, this time with great success.

This is us, the average human. We generally accept the so-called facts available about ourselves, and inertia carries us in the appropriate direction until someone or something gives us new facts. This holds two problems. First, it's passive. We're waiting for others or the world to tell us what and who we are and what we are capable of. Second, it limits us to only what we are exposed to, and as we just went through, most of this was not of our choosing or under our control.

You see yourself only in relation to what you've experienced thus far. So when you find a desire to go from $50,000 a year in annual earnings to $150,000 and you want to get motivated and driven, it's fairly hollow. You have no context for seeing yourself as someone who provides enough value to go from earning $4,166 per month to $12,500. You have no context for having so much money that you can pay for everyone's dinner on a night out, upgrade your home or furnishings, drive a car you are proud of, and jet off to whatever vacation you like. And yet you're trying to be a driven person committed to this new idea for yourself.

The idea must have some roots to it if you are going to really become driven and actually achieve it. I find these roots can come in two ways. First, how we see ourselves and what we are capable of. Take captive any goal you have and consider whether you truly see yourself doing what it takes to get there, and/or existing in the state of achieving it. You'll often be surprised to find some negative emotions and inability around it. This is where you dig in. You don't need a coach yelling, "You gotta want it more!" You just need to consider the truth of your want in relation to your level of desire and belief. Can you see yourself doing the work to triple your income and being the person who has such a great level of money and financial capacity? Can you see yourself doing the work to lose all the weight and be someone who looks fit and trim? Can you see yourself doing the work to start a side business and then being someone who is self-employed and calling all your own shots on a daily basis?

This is where we often find ourselves pushing and pulling and frustrated with ideals we really don't believe or can't viably conceive are possible for ourselves. An interesting exercise is to make a case for why you can't achieve the goal. We will be covering specific ways to change those beliefs.

How do you get driven when you don't believe in yourself and can't envision how you'll do it or what it will be like to achieve it? That calls for you to be fairly convinced you simply must do it, regardless. This is the foundation of so many hero movies. They weren't about characters who did the deep work to believe in themselves, but instead something happened requiring them to stand up and respond or face possible tragic consequences. I've seen someone triple their income in a short amount of time in response to the dire financial needs of a loved one. I've seen someone do a 180 on their health after getting a diagnosis stating that if they don't, they will possibly die and leave their loved ones bereft. I've seen many businesses come to fruition because someone became convinced they must solve a problem in the world they cared about.

Figure out how to envision yourself doing and achieving the goal, or find a reason why the goal must happen regardless. And if you didn't catch it by now, this is simply another perspective on fourth gear about manipulating the power of your emotions, as your emotions make up more of your beliefs than objective reality and "belief" do.

REVERSE: THE GREATEST ADVERSARY OF YOUR INDIVIDUAL DRIVE

In 1962 *Candid Camera* brought social conformity to the limelight with an episode called "Face the Rear," testing the experiments of Polish psychologist Solomon Asch on the power of blindly conforming to a majority group. In the episode, the *Candid Camera* crew waited for someone to enter an elevator and had a group of people enter with him and all face the rear of the elevator with their backs to the door. What followed were varying degrees of uncomfortable and confused responses from the unknowing elevator participant as they dealt with the pressure of conforming to the group. Some turned partially toward the back, some fully, and some even joined in completely as the group changed which direction they faced multiple times.

A more apt title for the episode would be "Face the Fear." A core need of ours is to belong and be accepted. It's arguably the strongest urge within us, and we often don't give it the gravity it deserves. When I was working with my friend Dr. Randy James in his Functional Medicine practice, the power of wanting to belong came to light for us. Time after time he would take in a new patient who was suffering from some pathology that had grown over time, and invariably the treatment he prescribed involved a life change—eating more healthfully, exercising, getting better sleep, working to have less stress. What we realized was that if left to themselves, most people could and would make drastic alterations to their lifestyle. They would change their normal dietary intake. They would restructure their daily schedule to accommodate for exercise and movement. They would meditate and trade late-night TV and chips for a candle, a book, and some tea. So why didn't they all? Social pressure.

These patients left the office with good intentions and willpower, yet they faced challenges as soon as they got home. They had to contend with roommates, spouses, and kids who might not want to have veggies constitute the majority of dinner with a small amount of meat and even less or no carbs. This can incite rebellion or a riot, especially if you have staunch "meat and potatoes" family members. To get up earlier than everyone else to go to the gym or take your office lunch break to run will likely get you questioned, if not teased. Going to bed an hour earlier than normal while everyone is engaged in the nightly entertainment ritual can be treated as if you're going AWOL. Time and time again it was this pressure that caused people to falter on their otherwise good intent.

Why this is important is that it shows us where the fight is. Instead of the usual focus on the person's commitment, self-discipline, and willpower, we must address how people can change among those around them who expect and often desire for them to remain the same. Not that those who love them wish them ill will, but they want to belong and be accepted just as much, and part of this is wanting others to stay just like them as well. A further issue comes when one member of a group strives to do something deemed better and it highlights others in the group wanting to stay where they are, and the change instills an actual feeling of threat.

Therefore for you to work out what you truly want and are driven to do, you must decide how you will face this resistance, or you will succumb to it. I have one primary prescription for you: Don't try to go against the flow. Find a different flow.

I'm not saying you should leave your family and ditch your friends, although growing in a positive direction may in fact force you to reconsider some specific relationships and even groups. Your greatest source of power is to find people who support and align with the direction you want to go in. This may sound like common sense, but we find that common sense is seldom common.

Please hear this: in any area of life we are about to address, your greatest opportunity is to align with as many people as you can who are going the same direction you desire to travel. Nobody really wants to go against the flow, as again, we long to belong. So don't fight the flow you're in—just jump over into a flow going the appropriate direction. You don't have to be superhuman, you just need to find the right flow.

ASSEMBLING YOUR DRIVE

You have the ingredients within you to be driven toward whatever objective you desire. You have just as much drive as anyone else, and this will help flesh out why you are flourishing in some areas of your life but not others. Where you may find yourself lacking is in one or more of the gears already discussed. However, just listing them out conceptually is like explaining how to drive a stick shift inside a classroom. We can discuss it and simulate it, and you could get straight As on explaining the dynamics, but you will not know how to actually drive a stick shift until you sit in the driver's seat and put the clutch in with one foot, feather the gas with the other, put the car in gear, and see if you can tactically get it right. In Part Two of this book, we'll walk through the key categories of life desire and fulfillment and learn how the gears play out as you shift each for yourself.

So far, we've been sitting in Driving 101 together, where I've taken you through some of the myths surrounding the concept of driven people, as well as offering ways you can, in fact, create all the drive you want in your own life right away.

In Chapters 3 through 9, we'll leave the confines of the classroom for the actual driving course. It's time to get in, buckle up, and start shifting through the gears of your own life. You are about to drive through the life-changing terrain most people never take the time to traverse. But you are not most people. I've compiled seven areas where I think most of us try to find fulfillment in our lives, but where we often take a wrong turn.

While these seven areas are not listed in order of importance, I placed them in a deliberate sequence. Resist the urge to skip ahead, or you will miss out on the key insights necessary to discern your true desires in later chapters. For instance, if you jump to "Work" without first considering "Purpose," you won't be fully equipped to dig deep into these areas of your life. So I encourage you to give each category your full attention, and work through some of the questions I pose in the "Take Action" sections. This is about you and for you. Let's begin!

CHAPTER SUMMARY

▶ We all have the ingredients to be fully driven, but like fingerprints, no two people have the same ingredients making up their unique recipe for drive. The purpose of this book is to discern what ingredients you have and how to build them into the right vehicle for you.

▶ You can theoretically "do anything," but you won't do everything well. Your specific makeup of drive ingredients is unique and finite, which is a good thing. Being told you can do anything and have no limits is errant and demotivating. You have specific propensities and the ability to be masterful with them. But it's not unlimited.

▶ Your capability and drive are made up of your (1) genetics, (2) environment, (3) individual and unique desires, (4) individual and unique motives, and (5) beliefs, which come from your values and faith.

▶ The number one enemy and obstacle to your authentic drive is cultural pressure—things you feel you should do and expectations you and others have put on you that aren't true to your personal makeup. You must become aware and let go of these handicapping pressures.

▶ Your drive is built intentionally, not by happenstance, which is the best news you can have.

PART TWO

DRIVING LESSONS

CHAPTER 3

What Drives
Your Purpose

You Are What You Have Faith In

I n July 2015, archaeologists discovered what are believed to be the oldest writings in the ancient city of Göbekli Tepe, in southeast Turkey. Göbekli Tepe is believed to contain the world's first temple, complete with a 12,000-year-old pictograph depicting a Buddhist funeral practice of sky burial, where a deceased human body is placed on a mountaintop to be eaten by scavenging animals. A majority of humankind's early pictographs and hieroglyphics similarly depict images related to faith and spirituality as the primary focus.

Throughout the span of history, humans have been drawn to powers bigger than us, and to stories that give us a clue to being part of more than what we experience here on Earth. It has not escaped my notice that out of the 200 influential guests I've had on my podcast, 99 percent profess placing faith in something greater than themselves and identify this greater purpose as a (if not *the*) primary driver for all they accomplish. If faith in a greater power is cited by 99 out of 100 of the world's most influential people, it would seem we should give that as much attention as we do their teachings on business and success, as it speaks beyond what they do and gets to the root of why they do it.

Let me be clear: this chapter is not about religion per se, and to tell the truth, it's not even about spirituality. Instead, the intent is to lend gravity to the incredibly powerful motive of having a greater reason for existence than simply serving yourself. In his podcast, Rabbi Daniel Lapin said, "Happiness is not the opposite of depression, the opposite of depression is purpose."[1] And theologian Frederick Buechner said, "Purpose is the place where your deep gladness and the world's deep hunger meet." Translation: the spark of drive is derived from having a purpose, and humanity finds its greatest purpose in serving other people. This isn't altruistic but intrinsically selfish, which is OK—we are naturally a selfish people. Yet serving only ourselves is the way of death, whereas we can find our greatest life in serving others. Thus, whether the purpose you have—the cause you believe in and fight for—is saving the environment, saving animals, saving democracy, or saving souls, it's not *what* you are saving that really matters. Anything other than saving your own butt will do nicely as a powerful motive that will fuel your drive.

A popular criticism of spirituality is that it's merely a man-made construct to give hope and explain the unknown—a placebo. There are scores of medical trials proving placebos can often be as effective as any primary treatment, and I'd have to agree. My brain believing I'm going to heal is over-all stronger medicine than any pharmaceutical. Again, our focus is not *what* you put faith in, but rather in showcasing *how* faith can be a profound driver. I didn't place this chapter on purpose and faith first because it's more important than the other factors we'll cover. However, experience has shown me what we believe about our life's purpose is ultimately the foundation for everything else we do. It's our core *why*.

To reference humanitarian Lynne Twist from Chapter 1 again, when I had her on my podcast we discussed how her commitment to The Hunger Project, something larger than herself, caused her to sense the world in a whole new way. She began to see herself differently and be liberated from the pettiness of her self-image and the culture. Her awareness of and commitment to her purpose crafted her into the person who could make the massive impact she has achieved across the globe. Let's revisit the story arc of our greatest movies: Life is going along as normal and then hits a snag—an event that causes trouble: Donald Miller's "inciting incident." Amid the chaos this incident has provoked, the hero has faith and devotion to a greater good. There are usually characters alongside the hero who don't care about any purpose beyond saving their own butts. These figures serve to elevate the hero's status and valor. Real life is no different. We all revere heroes who have a higher calling, while we look down on those who serve their own selfish ends. To that degree, serving others and a higher purpose and giving devotion to something beyond self is a prerequisite for being a hero. Nothing else constitutes hero status.

Don't miss the weight of this—it's not what you put faith in, and it's not what purpose you choose. The power is simply in you having faith in something greater than yourself. Many people are prone to shun any religious trappings, and claim their faith or spirituality is simply *love*, with the intention of giving this love to others. Those who find the most tangible traction here do so by applying love in a manner authentic to who they are (what Buechner calls "deep gladness") and a relevant human or cultural application (Buechner refers to this as "the world's deep hunger"). Now let's look at how to find your own authentic, deep gladness.

TAKE ACTION

A primary driver of your life is your purpose, which can lead to ultimate fulfillment. What you put faith in is bigger than you. Do you have faith or devotion to anything beyond yourself? If so, give it a sentence or two. If not, then you're now aware of a void in your life and can open the door for consideration as you continue reading. Either way you are now gaining ground beyond this aspect of your life being completely absent.

HOW GENETICS AFFECT YOUR PURPOSE

Neuroplasticity has come to the forefront of psychology in recent years, and rightly so. Where we used to consider the brain as a fixed entity, we now realize it is infinitely programmable, just like a computer. It can learn and grow and create new paths. This also hints at our brains' genetic predispositions. We know if your ancestors spent their lives eating a certain diet, you will likely function better on those foods. If they lived in a certain climate, you may find yourself feeling better in a similar setting. By the same token, the neuro pathways your ancestors created will have an impact on your brain's "set point"—your innate propensity, comfort level, and innate drive toward something. Think of it as a predisposition.

A simple analogy is simply thinking of a map of America. A wedding is announced in Maine. Some family members are close by in Vermont, so attending the wedding is no big deal. Others are nearby in Ohio and North Carolina. There are some other friends who live in Arizona and Washington, and one down in the Florida Keys, a much bigger trip. That is still not as arduous as the attendees who live in Hawaii and France. Sure, all these people can get to the wedding, but with such differing "set points" or places of origin, what will be a lovely day trip and a little gas for some will be a weeklong ordeal costing thousands for others. All are capable, but the effort and cost will be greater for some.

Do you come from generations of people who woke up every morning devoted to a great purpose that kept them fulfilled? This would lend itself toward a feeling of assurance that someone or something had their back, and their welfare wasn't all on them. Again, even if what they believed is contrary to your personal belief, think about the positive mental aspects this type of security provided. They were likely to live lives of greater inspiration, depth, and peace. A culture of this type would probably be one where this deeper meaning was just a part of the fabric of life, and they may have had a fair level of abundance overall. In 2015, researchers at the London School of Economics and Erasmus University Medical Center in the Netherlands found that evidence of sustained happiness, higher than the average levels, comes from participation in religion. Mauricio Avendano is an epidemiologist and author in the study and cited it may not be the religion itself but the sense of belonging and social inclusion that brings benefits.[2] This speaks again to the core of spirituality and being part of something greater than self. Thus, your natural set point may be to have a greater tendency to be drawn to a life of faith and even joy simply because you come from generations of more spiritual people.

On the flip side, you may come from people who had great hardship and poverty, whose days and lives were devoted to mere survival. There was no time to think about others much, or about a bigger picture and greater good, as all energy was reserved for just getting by. This mindset is not only for war-torn, developing countries but could be seen in any city where you'd find poverty, abuse, and relative isolation. In these places, the likely mantra would be, *nobody has my back, it's all on me, and I can rely on nobody and nothing.* Could you really conceive of serving a purpose beyond yourself in this kind of environment? What kind of neural pathways would this existence build?

In considering how your own genetics have driven your perspective on faith and purpose, try to determine where your set point might be. Does it lean toward the light of faith and purpose? Or do you tend toward the gloomier picture of "every person for themselves"? Once you are more aware of your natural tendencies, you can then take steps to start reworking (or rejecting!) the neural pathways you were born with. Great strides in neuro and cognitive therapy and training have been made in recent years, and the results have motivated inclusion of such treatments by therapists and coverage from insurance companies. Today brain-training and brain-mapping providers can be found in most major cities.

TAKE ACTION

How have your genetics driven your perspective on faith and purpose? In considering what you know of the three biological generations behind you, would you deem your genetic set point for faith and purpose is helping or hurting your drive? How? Now how can you move forward accordingly?

HOW ENVIRONMENT
AFFECTS YOUR PURPOSE

I've already mentioned my own Amish heritage on my dad's side. He grew up in an intrinsically strict and narrow religious structure. In our popular culture that's continually obsessed with the tension between the so-called conservatives and liberals, I have to say that it doesn't get any more conservative than the Amish. My dad left those stark, religious confines, but I still grew up in the Bible Belt of Kentucky with my early years spent entrenched in the walls of the Southern Baptist church, where I adhered to the construct of Christianity. I am as fluent in such religion as I am in cycling. I've toed up to the line of over 1,000 competitive bike races and possibly twice as many church services! While today I have much concern around organized religion, I still give a lot of credit to the power of my own faith. In my own experience, I find that those who have been exposed to a culture of faith showcase more peace and fulfillment. Seeing my parents' unshakable devotion to a morality that's based upon service planted in me a lifelong desire to be of value to others and looking beyond myself. It's not a sales pitch, but the sharing of evidence-based experience.

Think of how your own parents or primary caregivers conveyed their faith to you, whether in subtle or overt ways. Could they have created pathways in your mind and heart? Again, the focus here is not religion. Whether you were fed a huge dose of religion during your upbringing, or your caretakers weren't religious people at all, does not necessarily place much bearing on your overall view of a greater purpose, and therefore your capacity for an internal faith drive. After all, your folks could have been uber-devoted to a religion with no true heart, or conversely, they may never have stepped foot in a church yet joyfully devoted their lives to service to others and the planet. What we want to discern is the spirit you were surrounded by, and where it left you in regard to finding a greater purpose beyond your own little world.

This is a time to consider the threads of what you witnessed of your parents' or caregivers' worldview. Was the world a beautiful place to them, or a disappointment? Did things work out in general, or did they always feel like they got the shaft? Were they encouraging to other people or critical? Were they humble or prideful? Gracious or judgmental? Did they feel fortunate or victimized? This is not about circumstances or relationships, but the beliefs behind them.

Also consider whether your family ties were strong or weak. Was devotion to family important? Was providing for the family treated as a chore or an honor? Like I said before, the answers do not absolutely determine your capacity for great faith and the drive that ensues, but they do influence your base set point.

TAKE ACTION

How has your environment driven your faith? In considering your upbringing and the primary caretakers and influential people in your life, would you deem your set point for faith as helping or hurting your drive? How? For those of you with little to no inclination and quite possibly feelings of animosity toward spirituality, I encourage you to step back from your current predisposition against it, or an environmental (upbringing) trauma you hold against it, and give yourself freedom to authentically consider it for yourself.

ROADBLOCKS TO AVOID

There is a song by The Unlikely Candidates called "Follow My Feet" that has two converse lines telling the story of a friend who "lies and steals and cheats" and culminates by stating he must do what he has to do in order to get what he wants, and "If I don't take it, somebody else will." This is juxtaposed with another friend who "loves humanity" and desires to help the poor and ill and then sums up his feelings by stating, "If I don't do it, nobody will." I often see this differing perspective regarding purpose in business owners, where some view it as a game to get people's money and others as a service they desire to offer. It would be stereotypical for me to say the latter make more money than the former, but it's simply not true. If your goal is to get people's money, you can do it, no different than a pickpocket. The greater cost is to the soul, even though your bank account may be full.

There are three primary detours that often derail the glorious drive of greater purpose: a victim mentality, a scarcity mentality, and judgment of purpose. Everyone is victimized by something; not everything that happens to us is of our choosing or within our control, whether it be abuse or a car wreck or realities far less traumatic. But there is a huge difference between being victimized and *living* as a victim. We all know people who are defined and constrained by the tragedies that have befallen them, and others who are victorious because of those same tragedies. This in no way minimizes anyone's suffering, but simply points to what some people do in response to it, and the person they become as a result. The easiest way to audit yourself is to see whether you tend to blame others or outside forces for your lack, or if you take responsibility and ownership. Simply said and seldom done. Personal development guru Tom

Bilyeu has a short video clip called "It's All Your Fault," where he exaggerates this concept by saying that if a meteorite comes out of the sky and crashes through his bedroom and kills his wife, he will know it is all his fault.[3] This is a preposterous claim but exaggerates the idea that accepting anything else gives power to something or someone else and requires us to live as victims.

We as humans, me included, avoid blame like the plague. More and more, we are living in a blameless culture, accepting less responsibility for the plights and predicaments of our lives, and pointing the finger at anything and everything—except ourselves. In doing this, we give away the only power we have: our own agency. To circle back to Tom's dramatic statement, he means that while the meteorite couldn't be his fault, the way he responds is. He could lament his wife's death and sue the roofing company or the cosmos. In the thralls of grief, he could choose to end his own life, figuratively or literally. Or he can give thanks for the glorious gift of his time on Earth with his wife and carry on in gratitude. Maybe he devotes himself to the purpose of a meteorite tracking systems or improved roofs and makes another fortune. But you can't live in a victim mentality and be driven by a greater purpose to serve humanity and the world—you can't serve a world you believe is just out to get you.

Similar to this is a scarcity mentality, often referenced today as a "zero-sum game." Simply stated, if Bobby has a lollipop and gives it to Mary, he receives a loss and she receives a gain. This is a one-dimensional outlook: if you've ever experienced a child proactively giving to another of their own accord, you've also seen that the gift of giving provides far more to the giver than to the recipient. I have adopted daughters, and my wife and I are often told that they are so lucky that we adopted them and "saved their precious little lives." To us, that feels so shameful, as we know the people whose lives were saved the most were our own. I'll admit I'm not a natural giver, and I'm not uber-compassionate. But my girls helped birth so much compassion and grace in me and broke down so much of my judgment and criticism toward others. For every ounce I've given to them, I've received tenfold benefit. Adopting them may be one of the most self-supporting things I've ever done. I'm not saying this to make some self-righteous statement or take a holier-than-thou pose. But I am selfish enough to know a zero-sum game and scarcity mentality serves me far less than a win-win. So, take a good, hard look at your own perspective, and you may find the root issues that either fuel or deplete your drive from a greater purpose.

Up next is judgment of purpose. My brother Jared spent a decade in Africa helping to rescue women and children out of sex slavery. At the same time, I was working in America speaking to and working with middle- and upper-class people whose main challenges would be fairly labeled as "First World problems." I grappled with this for a while, striving to justify my choice of work and ultimately concluded that I was also helping people, just in very different circumstances. I also realized that my purpose and passion is right here: writing, podcasting, and speaking to you, the type of person who aspires to do good with your life. I may help inspire and equip you to serve in a developing country and do my part in this capacity.

Don't judge your cause or the purpose of others. The greatest power of humanity is having a purpose at all, and I believe a primary reason for the decline in today's mental health is the lack of purpose and the general malaise of people who don't participate and engage in life, but simply spectate and experience it virtually. I can't stress this point enough: the power is in *having* a purpose, not what the purpose is.

TAKE ACTION

Before this Take Action section begins, I want to take a moment to acknowledge that there are absolutely situations in which you may have been the victim and that you should never take the blame for what happened to you. In those horrible situations, the most important thing you can do is find compassion for yourself in order to find peace. And I hope you do find that compassion and peace.

What I'd like to work through together here is different. These are situations in which you have felt victimized but everything could have played out differently had you responded differently. For example, if you have been laid off from a job because of something like a buyout, did you assume the victim mentality and not look for a new job for months, or did you quickly reorient yourself and find another opportunity? The difference in those two responses is tremendous—and those reactions are entirely in your control.

Despite how it may sometimes feel in the moment, you do have a great amount of control in how you respond. Going back to our example of losing a job, if you were to take on a nonvictim and abundance mentality, you might see the situation as an opportunity to consider a more interesting, fitting, and lucrative job, or maybe you'd finally pursue that business idea you've often pondered.

When you find yourself in victim mode, take a step back and take a moment to be present and get out of reaction mode. Considering these aspects of mental roadblocks and working to adopt a perspective of responding, abundance, and being nonjudgmental of your desires will set you up to orient yourself more quickly and effectively when trials arise.

WHAT YOU WANT TO HAVE PURPOSE IN

With the aforementioned call to not judge the value of a purpose, we can now deftly open the door to asking, "What purpose really speaks to your head, your heart, and your soul?" Is it on the homeless row or in the White House? A trash-strewn dirt street or Wall Street? A church or a spaceship? A person, a country, an animal, or an institution?

What you are passionate about is the sexy term that gets all the press, but there is even more relevance in considering what breaks your heart. It's fascinating to be in social situations and find what interests people and what moves them, if anything. Eleanor Roosevelt is credited with stating, "Great minds discuss ideas, average minds discuss events, and small minds discuss people." On one hand I agree, if we're talking about the worldview and interests of someone who devotes their time to discussing ideas to serve humanity, versus merely gossiping and criticizing people. On the other hand, this sentiment may impede someone's natural propensity toward a purpose. Those discussing people may want to serve them face-to-face. Those discussing events may find working with groups is more fitting, while the idea-prone people may tend toward serving from behind the scenes to develop methodologies that others can effectively employ. This perspective can free you up to serve in whatever manner floats your boat, so to speak. Don't get derailed trying to justify it—if it's purpose-filled and focused on others, you are good.

Back in my church days, we'd question who had more value: Billy Graham who saved a million souls for God, or the missionary in the African bush who saved three. The question itself reveals our propensity to judge the value of contributions. So again, don't. Go and be you.

You may know what purpose plucks your heartstrings, and if so, I'm imploring you to take it seriously and not discount it for any reason. But if you don't have the foggiest idea of what your purpose is, you now have the fun of gaining exposure to various options. There should be at least some threads of interests you can follow. Is it environmental or cultural? Politics or spirituality? Animals, resources, or space? And whatever it is it does not have to stay the same for the rest of your life. My brother, who was devoted to serving humanity from the trenches of Rwanda, now serves humanity in the advocacy of space exploration. He went from working among those in poverty to working alongside billionaires, but he doesn't feel a double standard as it's just different sides of the same service. Who knows what platform he'll be involved in in another decade? But you can bet it will still carry his core thread of purpose.

TAKE ACTION

What interests you? What are you passionate about, or what breaks your heart? Pay attention to your answers. There is a cause that needs you, and you need that purpose in order to support the foundation of your drive.

WHAT MOTIVATES YOUR PURPOSE?

As you clarify your faith and purpose, this is the time to really consider your motive. Is it fear, pain, expectations of others, desire, or pride? What is the emotion behind your drive here? The point is not to judge it but to make sure you are aware of and in agreement with it.

Around 1997 I met my dear friend Ronnie Freeman. He'd just graduated college and was waiting tables at a restaurant and writing and performing music on the side. Music was his love. He brought a keyboard to my house and played a couple of songs and sheepishly gave me a little cassette tape with three songs on it. I was blown away by his music and talent. I, of course, asked him where he was going with it, and he cited his personal struggle with knowing how much being on stage and receiving applause meant to him, and in battling his pride and ego he was going to forgo a pursuit of music. I flat-out said there was no way he was keeping his great gift from the world by denying it. His ego was a problem he'd just have to deal with. (In the ensuing years, I've had to grapple with this same issue myself, and needed the same counsel.)

Today Ronnie is a renowned singer and songwriter who has penned songs sung by top recording artists and is hired to perform at events around the country. One of his greatest attributes was awareness at an early stage of his life of what his purpose was and the motives behind it. While Ronnie knew part of his motive was pride and feeding his ego, his motive to bless and lift people's lives was much stronger. He did both. Especially mine.

Anthony de Mello was a teacher, writer, Jesuit priest, and psychotherapist. In his book *Awareness*, a personal favorite of mine, he claims there is no such thing as selflessness. "I give something, I get something," says de Mello. "That isn't charity, that's enlightened self-interest." In religious spheres we often hear of the call to give selflessly and to die to self. But Anthony says that's impossible, and I agree. Like Ronnie, in pursuing a true purpose and calling, a healthy and effective individual will find they are jointly serving themselves and others. You could even say, serving themselves through serving others. Going back to the zero-sum game versus a win-win scenario, it's OK if both you and those you serve get benefit. We tend to try to discount an effort if we know it's feeding our appetite for self-grandeur. Like Ronnie, we will need to moderate and constantly monitor and manage this urge to keep it in check.

You may have seen someone pursue a purpose with good intentions and get derailed by personal gain. It happens. And yet you'll find few if any people doing any greater good who aren't benefiting themselves as well. I'm so grateful the likes of Mother Teresa, Gandhi, and Martin Luther King Jr. didn't let their notoriety and unavoidable personal gain keep them from their purpose. Good leaders will bring in peers for accountability to keep them from getting too focused on themselves.

To you, then, what is motivating your interest and passion and broken heart, and do you agree with it? Can you balance and manage it? Can you harness it?

A great exercise is to fill in the blank after the words, "So that. . . ." For example, *I want to help serve/help/advocate for X, so that. . . ."* What is the desire you want to fulfill for others? What is the problem you want to solve? What is the joy you want to provide or pain you want to help alleviate?

And if you can't quite connect to a service, which is often more difficult the younger you are and having not yet experienced much of life, then just focus on your interests. If you can state the interest and give a why, that's even better. But if all you can come up with is a mere interest, it's still a great start. My 16-year-old son is really interested in biology but can't yet conceptualize a strong why, and this is OK. Right now we just support the interest and let him gain exposure so his purpose can eventually come to fruition.

Here are some relevant motivating emotions and feelings to help jog your mind for this and all categories:

Positive Feelings and Descriptors	Negative Feelings and Descriptors
Excited	Resentful
Hopeful	Resigned
Curious	Bitter
Committed	Fearful
Missional	Drudgery
Contributing	Imprisoned
Helping	Bored
Important	Numb
Valiant	Irrelevant
Grateful	Bullied
Inspired	Controlled
Fulfilled	Belittled
Altruistic	Chained

TAKE ACTION

What is motivating what you want for your faith and purpose? What emotions do you feel? What circumstances are part of your why?

SEE YOURSELF THERE

In the movie *The Matrix*, when Neo takes the red pill and ends up in the matrix construct, he realizes he's clothed and looking a certain way. The character Morpheus says it's his residual self-image. We all have this, a way we naturally see ourselves. Motivation expert and ex-NFL player Anthony Trucks says before we can go forth achieving a goal, we need an identity shift (also the name of his book) to match up our self-image to the reality of achieving a goal. We seldom address this step, so we find ourselves clamoring for success because at our core we can't envision ourselves as the person who has achieved something at a higher level than we've been before.

It can feel a bit audacious to state you are committing to any aspect of faith and platform of purpose if you haven't done it before. Remember, it's not a tattoo for all the world to see. I know many people who keep their core reasons very private and personal. How you express your faith and purpose is a matter completely separate from what you choose and commit to, and it's the latter we give focus to here.

Asking if you can see yourself achieving your goal can bring up some significant difficulties regarding your self-image. On one hand, it's beneficial to try to envision yourself as someone who can profess their purpose to the world. But it's not a requirement. You can also strive to envision yourself as someone who is quietly and privately pursuing this core purpose and being driven by it. My personal spiritual faith is more important to me as something that always guides me and often most acutely when I'm alone. If social engagement was primarily motivating my efforts, I wouldn't consider it a very solid faith that can provide peace and long-term fulfillment.

Regarding your purpose, depending on what it is, it may require or benefit from public proclamation, or not. The 200 guests on my show all had a purpose they were devoted to, and some of them were as plain as the titles of their books. Zig Ziglar's initial fame and influence came from his expert guidance in sales and business, and he used it to draw people to a life of purpose, devotion, and faith. People bought *Secrets of Closing the Sale* by the millions to help their business success, but leaders like Seth Godin read it over and over for how it gave guidance on living a great life. Can you envision yourself being the person who feels a higher calling in life and lives each day with purpose? Who attaches this purpose to your identity? I often find people who have a purpose they care about and believe in but are reticent to really attach themselves to it. They may think it goes against their self-image, or they may face scrutiny within their social circles. People used to take more pride in their heritage, what country and state they lived in, and what faith they held. While I'm not lobbying for everyone to stake claims to their identity to the world, I do find an aspect of success related to those who are at peace with what they are all about. Take two people who strongly believe in a nutritional diet of life-sustaining foods for themselves, others, and the planet, but only one attaches healthy eating to their identity and the other doesn't. My experience is the former will find more sustainable success. We best support the things we tangibly associate with. Which harkens back to the tattoo. Maybe I should finally get one!

Now there is a caveat to this aspect of envisioning that I'll refer to in every subsequent chapter in this book: conviction. Let's say you can't truly envision yourself at the end goal. You can still be so committed to having it happen that you just do it anyway. Remember George Bailey in the holiday movie classic *It's A Wonderful Life*, when he's considering ending his life by jumping off a bridge, and then the angel Clarence jumps in and cries for help? Nothing changed in George's belief about himself and his own circumstances. He just saw someone in need, and his submission to death instantly changed to a resolution for life.

I won bike races because I believed I could. I could see myself doing what it takes and standing on the podium. But when I lived in a 2,200-square-foot modular home on the Colorado tundra, bursting at the seams with five kids (one slept in a closet), and we had a desire for a glorious home for them, I didn't really see myself building and living in a big custom home in the woods. I'd never experienced one iota of building a home and living in a greater style. But I felt a huge desire for my kids to grow up in a better place than where we were. So we plowed forward, one part courage and one part stupidity. But the pain of not having this new reality for my kids was greater than my lack of knowledge and belief.

A great way to foster this type of perspective is to flip the script on considering the risk of going after something, and instead focus on the risk of *not* going after it. Are you OK if another year goes by and X doesn't happen? If you are in the same place then as you are now? How will you feel about yourself in a year? If you can involve someone else's benefit into the equation, you'll find much more power. I often have endeavors where my desire and belief aren't strong enough, but if it involves the welfare of and benefit to my family, I'll find the motive and drive to do it. Who else will benefit from you achieving success in a given area? Who else will suffer or miss out if you don't? This isn't an effort to embrace guilt or expectations of others—you still own the endeavor for yourself. But sometimes when we struggle with enough motive in benefiting ourselves, we can find it in benefiting others.

Apply these concepts in the chapters that follow. Regarding a faith and a purpose, if you just can't see yourself or identify with being someone with a proclaimed devotion to it, can you find a strong enough conviction to go after it anyway?

Let me be candid. I have a broken heart for a problem I see in our culture today with the cataclysmic rise in chronic illness and disease in America and want to find a solution that at least makes a dent in alleviating it. The concept is so big and grandiose, however, that I must admit I can't really see how to make it happen and what my exact role can be. I've tried to shelve it over the years, but I just can't quite leave it behind. So, I'm trusting it to come about eventually, and I just keep taking baby steps forward. It's a purpose I'm committed to and am acting on, even though I struggle to claim it with confidence and envision it for myself.

TAKE ACTION

Can you see yourself having the faith and purpose you desire? Or do you have enough conviction to act regardless?

YOUR PURPOSE ZONES

In researcher and explorer Dan Buettner's 2012 bestselling book *The Blue Zones*, he researched nine places where the people seemed to live the longest and revealed their secrets to help us all live healthier lives. His main takeaway from his world travels was that the healthiest and happiest people are part of cultures that are inherently . . . (guess what?) healthy and happy. This offers a hint at how you can grow comfortable in your faith and purpose: find others to commune with. I have yet to find a particular faith or purpose that doesn't have communities and groups to align with. In this day and age, we have immediate access to nearly all the information the world holds, for free. I'm not one to network and join a social group, but I'll turn to books and videos to hear from specific people in the space. Whatever your flavor, there are "zones" to join.

I've had numerous guests on my shows who cite the powerful impact of reading biographies of their heroes and leaders in their desired areas of faith and purpose. Biographies and autobiographies are tremendous for lifting the mystique around certain figures and making our heroes more relatable. We can get deeper perspectives on how they accomplished their goals, while we find ourselves gaining comfort and confidence in accomplishing our own.

Today we also have documentaries and reality shows that, while generally overdramatizing things, will give you relevant exposure to the spirit of the direction you are interested in. You can also go for it and engage in real time. Read books on the subject, listen to podcasts, find events in your area—the resources and opportunities have never been more available than they are today.

Perhaps most importantly, I've found it can often take just one person to give you the supportive zone you want, which is why we often find people's greatest encouragement comes from a spouse, sibling, family member, or close friend.

TAKE ACTION

Where is your faith and purpose zone? Where might you find it? Make a list and don't discount anything or anyone.

CHAPTER SUMMARY

▶ **Case for Faith:** Having faith in a bigger picture and greater purpose than yourself is a primary motive of drive and has been for the span of humanity. If you want a foundation of drive that can carry you toward ultimate life fulfillment, clarifying and devoting to a purpose in life is your greatest asset.

▶ **What Is Inherent:** People devoted to a purpose have said that it's kept them inspired and fulfilled, while their spirituality gave them assurance that someone or something had their back and they weren't alone.

▶ **What You've Been Exposed To:** How did your parents or caregivers tend to perceive their faith? Were you exposed to those who placed faith in anything other than self? Was life a gift or a burden? Was the world hedging in their favor or out to get them? Their outlook had a tremendous influence on your "set point," or your propensity to be able to think beyond your own world and needs.

▶ **Roadblocks to Avoid:** Blame and victim mentality will handicap your faith and ability to engage with a purpose, while responsibility and ownership will enable and equip you. Giving and serving should be seen as a win-win instead of a zero-sum game. Religious exposure and teaching could either support or sabotage you, depending on how you were raised. Be wary of judging the value of a purpose you are drawn to, and remember the real power is in having a purpose at all, not so much what the purpose is.

▶ **What You Authentically Want:** What are you passionate about? What is your heart broken by? What are you interested in? All these questions are valid and worthy. What speaks to your head, heart, and soul? Remember that your answers can and should evolve and grow. But the most important thing is to go forth and pursue these interests.

▶ **What Motivates You:** Your motives will undoubtedly be to serve yourself and others, but it's the combination and proper management of the two that will be pivotal to your success. Your core motive and driving emotion are not necessarily right or wrong, but it's crucial that you agree with them.

▶ **See Yourself There:** To embrace a faith or purpose is daunting, as it connects directly to your self-image and the very essence of your identity. You are best served not to strive to justify what it is. And you don't have to shout it from the rooftops or get a tattoo emblazoned on your arm. Though you can! What's key is that you find peace and comfort with how you attach yourself to your faith and purpose. If you can't see it but find a strong enough conviction to go after it, so be it! This too is valid.

▶ **Your Faith Zone:** Get with people or a person who embraces your chosen faith or purpose. Read biographies and memoirs. Watch documentaries. Read books. Exposing yourself to your areas of interest and people involved will do more for your confidence than anything.

CHAPTER 4

What Drives Your Relationships

You Are Who You Love

New York City proper covers 302.6 square miles and boasts a population of 8.8 million people, which results in 29,081 people per square mile. Everyone gets 958 square feet of space. To put this in perspective, the back deck of my house is 700 square feet. Now compare this with the entire country of Finland, which has a population of 5.5 million people and covers 130,672 square miles. This equates to only 42 people per square mile. The Finnish people theoretically each get 663,771 square feet of space to themselves! I live in a pretty big home, on acreage inside a national forest. I like my space. So I'm thinking the Finns are probably far happier and more at peace than the New Yorkers, right? They know how to be present and live at a slower pace and are veritable Zen masters, while the big city folk are anxious messes among the congested environment of their lives. And I'd be wrong.

A February 2021 press release by the Finnish Red Cross cites that one in three Finns suffer from loneliness.[1] To take it further, a 2016 paper was published by the American Public Health Association, which showcased another Finnish study revealing that social isolation was an acute predictor of mortality.[2] A layman's interpretation is basically that lonely, more solitary people experience increased adverse health conditions and die sooner. The Finns overall aren't flourishing from all the space they have, away from other people. They are suffering.

This may seem elementary, but if you think about it, the implications are profound. It makes sense that if you live by a nuclear power plant, you will likely develop negative health symptoms leading to an earlier death. Likewise, more and more studies are showcasing the danger of loneliness and isolation. And worse, living in New York City won't cure it either, as we have just as many isolated and disconnected people there, even as they rub shoulders and live in close proximity with other humans. In America, one of the fastest growing categories of chronic illness and disease is what is labeled as "diseases of despair," spiking even more during the Covid-19 pandemic. Apparently all the online connections and Zoom meetings didn't make up for a lack of face-to-face interactions in our lives and the dire necessity we all have to be in more intimate relationship with one another. Whether it's close friends or casual acquaintances, the energy of being together in the flesh has no comparison.

Australian hospice nurse Bronnie Ware, in her memoir *The Top Five Regrets of the Dying*, cited the number four deathbed regret as, "I wish I'd stayed in touch with my friends." In Daniel Pink's 2022 book *The Power of Regret*, he says that among *all* ages the number one category of regrets were those of connection. Relationships. Am I making my case here? We all give head nods to the importance of relationships, but we don't seem to grasp the tangible correlation to not only our happiness but our literal health, wellness, and quality of life.

While researching this topic I saw one of the many dystopian movies with some of my kids. These movies basically all have the same story line: something happens and a virus wipes out almost everyone, or we scorch the Earth and only a fraction of humanity is left. And we follow the story of one or two lone individuals seeking out . . . what? What is the entire point of the story? They aren't looking to loot the world in pursuit of gold, Porsches, or tacos. Instead, they are desperately seeking other people. It occurred to me, and I encourage you to ponder this as well, what if you woke up tomorrow morning and the Earth was just as it is. No changes. Except you are alone. Not another living soul or animal on the planet. But let's say the electricity is still running and you have full access to anything and everything. You can go find and eat any food you want. Go to the theater and binge-watch your favorite movies on the big screen indefinitely. Go grab the keys to any car on the Porsche lot and drive 150 miles per hour down Main Street. Commandeer a billionaire's yacht and anchor at a tropical beach. The world is truly your oyster.

The questions are: How long would you last? How long would this be fun? What I quickly realized is without other people I have absolutely no purpose and nothing is truly fun. My entire life only has meaning from relationships with others. It brought to mind the Trappist monk Thomas Merton, who spent so much of his life in solitude as a hermit, just him and God, and I questioned, actually judged initially, the value and validity of his choice for this lifestyle. I couldn't reconcile him sitting alone for months on end, just communing with God, and that having much purpose. Then I came to realize Merton had spent most of his time in solitude writing 54 books. His purpose was to positively influence and impact others. It was a remote relationship, but a relationship nonetheless. His purpose was found in serving other people.

It's not just nice to have friends and intimate relationships. It's absolutely vital. Nobody wakes up and thinks, *Gosh, I'm hungry. It would be nice to eat once in a while. But hey, I've got things to do. Other priorities right now. Maybe someday.* Yet this is how our culture treats real relationships, and we are starving ourselves to a death of our emotions and purpose.

TAKE ACTION

A primary driver of your life and ultimate fulfillment is your relationships. How would you rate your relationships? Not by number, but by quality. Intimacy? Frequency? Do you feel your relational status is helping or hurting your life? This is a good time to be honest and audit yourself.

HOW YOUR GENETICS VALUE RELATIONSHIPS

The highest grossing romantic comedy of all time is *My Big Fat Greek Wedding*, a 2002 independent film written by Nia Vardalos, who also performed the starring role of Toula. Nia based the story on her own family and her personal experience of marrying a non-Greek man. The film depicts Toula's oversized, very close-knit, and significantly dysfunctional family, where everyone is in each other's business. This strikes a stark contrast to her non-Greek boyfriend Ian, who is an only child and whose parents are described as "dry toast." It's not so much a sales pitch for a big family versus a small one but a tip toward relational intimacy and the sharing of the ups and downs of life and the value of interconnectedness.

So, do you come from relationships full of interconnectedness and strong relational ties, even if slightly dysfunctional, or is your lineage more "dry toast" and disconnected? The issue again isn't about family size or even the number of relationships, it is about tight and meaningful relationships and connectivity.

Everyone wants to know their genetic DNA and what ancestry they came from. They want testimony to who they are. But who you really are is not so much about your skin, eye, or hair color, but how you see and relate to others. How much more powerful to do the research to know who your ancestors were to other people. Did they have tight-knit and loving, or dispersed and contentious family relationships? Did they have friends, and were they avidly involved in their community? This will have far more impact on your actual life than color, height, or a propensity for juggling. A theme I'll be hitting in every chapter is "Genetics loads the gun and environment [i.e., your lifestyle] pulls the trigger." This is a quote attributed to Francis Collins, a physician-geneticist who discovered genes associated with a number of diseases, and who led the Human Genome Project. As I've said in previous chapters, you have some good and bad propensities loaded into your gun or burned onto your life CD regarding certain aspects of your life, but only you get to choose the lifestyle and decisions to pull the trigger on the outcome you desire.

Dysfunction, abuse, and divorce do not necessarily indicate a lack of relational value and drive, so don't let these realities make you feel you necessarily have a deficit. More troubling would be living in solitude, devoid of human engagement. We are looking to discern if "your people" made relationships a priority in their lives, and if those relationships were healthy and strong or distant and weak.

Psychologist Dr. Kevin Leman studied birth order for 35 years and authored *The Birth Order Book*. In it, he showcases how birth order alone can significantly impact our performance at work. Firstborn children for instance, statistically get more attention from their parents. The increased encouragement and resources often fosters more self-motivated and confident individual who often end up in leadership roles. However, the lack of siblings can also breed self-centeredness and difficulty in working with teams. While birth order could be more attributed to environmental factors covered next, if you come from a long line of single children or parents and grandparents who were first children, this can of course impact your set point.

TAKE ACTION

How have your genetics driven your relationship desires? In considering what you know of the three biological generations behind you, would you guess your genetic set point for relationships is helping or hurting your drive? How? Now how can you adjust accordingly?

HOW YOUR ENVIRONMENT VALUES RELATIONSHIPS

How were relationships treated in your upbringing? Were your parents or direct caretakers devoted to family? Was consistent communication and engagement a priority? Was it a healthy connection or a near violent bond like we see in depictions of the mafia? What about friends? Did your family have strong and devoted friendships outside of biological or traditional family makeups? Were other people involved in your family's life? Or was it the opposite? Was there little to no family involvement and possibly severe and specific rejection of such? Did you have parents or a single parent whose life was work, and maybe you, but really nobody else? No strong or even consistent friendships to speak of? All of these factors have tremendous influence on your relational set point, even if you've gone on to have close relationships.

We tend to find more inherent relational health and drive from people who were more entrenched with family and extended family than those who were not. The relational drive and expectations are statistically greater from those whose upbringing and young adulthood was rife with involvement and connection to grandparents, aunts and uncles, and cousins. Likewise, from those whose caregivers were often found communicating and sharing their lives consistently with friends. The exposure to relationships begets your familiarity, comfort, and expectation of having close and involved relationships.

Looking at how relationships figured in during challenging times can be telling as well. When things got hard, did you see your caregivers turning to others for encouragement, love, and support? Did they turn to anyone for counsel? Did they rely on relationships to help them in a time of need? Or was it the opposite altogether, and they isolated and turned in on themselves? It's likely you will unconsciously repeat whichever behaviors you were exposed to. Though sometimes people will fall on the other side and in response become codependent on others, which is not good either. The point is to become aware of your natural propensities.

Take a hard look at the overall outlook on relationships you were exposed to, as it will significantly influence some of your own relational set points and drive. The key word here is *influence*. Not direct or dictate. But were relationships valued and invested in, or was life a solitary journey for the most part?

TAKE ACTION

How has your environment influenced your relational drive? In considering your upbringing and the primary caretakers and influential people in your life, would you deem your environmental set point for relationships as helping or hurting your drive? How?

ROADBLOCKS TO AVOID

What relationships should you have to get the most fulfillment out of your life? Which ones, what should they look like, and how should they function? The greatest roadblocks to our unique relational drivers are our concepts of the "right ones." The expectations are that you should have a close gang of friends as a kid; then form college relationships lasting a lifetime; then get a spouse, who will become your primary life relationship; and then birth or adopt some kids and have a golden Rolodex of super-close friends and family.

There is precedent for these expectations, as we recognize the history of humanity as tribal. There is strength, safety, and meaning in a community. Regardless of your personality type or natural propensity, our ancestors were to some degree part of a "big fat Greek family," and individuals learned to function as such. People had to rely on each other for basic survival. We can look to this for some of our set points while also realizing that this concept has been wholly obliterated today. Those communities of yore were involved in daily tasks such as hunting and gathering and farming to ensure they'd have food, clothing, and shelter. Today, of course, we don't have to fight for our daily survival. We can pretty much get all we need for survival and beyond while working from a computer and never leaving our home or talking to another soul.

In terms of physical and economic survival, we no longer need to intrinsically rely on a community and relationships. And as we tend toward doing what is easiest and most convenient, relational investment has declined. During the Covid pandemic most of the working world figured out how to conduct their job and business without physical interaction. We met online and videoconferencing reached new levels. It harkens back to the holograms of *Star Trek* where we could virtually see and hear people in real time. From this we could surmise all was well. Yet a 2021 report from Harvard's Making Caring Common Project suggests that more than one in three Americans faced "serious loneliness" during the pandemic, including over 60 percent of young adults. For our emotional survival, purpose, and life fulfillment, deep relationships, with physical presence paramount, are absolutely vital. They are ultimately where we find purpose, and they are the primary crux of our drive. And thus, you see the problem.

While I've made a case for the profound value of relationships as core drivers of our life, I will not advocate for specific types of relationships, but rather, help you become aware of what to consider. But it's ultimately up to you. Not cultural expectations, but what drives and fulfills you, and allowing for it to be completely unique to you. Let's take a look at the key relationships of our lives and how they can block our drive if we aren't aware and in agreement with how we perceive and position them.

Yourself

I credit Robin Sharma, bestselling author of *The Everyday Hero Manifesto*, for bringing my attention to our relationship with ourselves as being the foundation for all our relationships. And the one we most often miss. In an episode of my podcast titled "Values, Motives, and Habits," I asked Robin about his relationships, and he stated his first priority is tending to the relationship he has with himself. This immediately resonated with me as wisdom, even though I'd never explicitly conceptualized it for myself. But now it seems so obvious. Of course, how can we have good, healthy, and fulfilling relationships with others if we don't first establish the same with ourselves? Not putting a relationship with yourself as priority number one is the primary roadblock to all of your relational health and drive. If you don't, it can create toxic ripple effects from the onset. If you look in the mirror with disdain, talk and think about yourself with disappointment and loathing, and distrust and disapprove of your own name, you are destined for unhealthy relationships and a codependent drive. My own relationships have intrinsically followed my view of myself and my own haphazard self-perception that swings between pride and disdain. This instruction to tend to the relationship with yourself first is possibly my number one answer to, "What would you tell yourself in your youth?" I'll speak to this a bit further in "What Motivates Your Relationships" later in this chapter.

Romantic Relationships

If aliens visited Earth and viewed the marketplace and heard our popular songs, they could quickly surmise that we're obsessed with romance, dating, and sex. I read that 60 percent of all songs ever written are about love, and one of the age-old adages of marketing is, of course, "sex sells." My life experience would confirm this. It would be interesting to see how much of all social media and advertising directly relates to an intimate relationship between two people. From this we could simply assume a romantic relationship with someone should be a key driver of our life. I won't attempt to counter this, but simply ask if it's true for you—at all, or right now. Does it have to be the main driver? Can you have a fulfilled life with only platonic relationships? Science would explain that our romantic drive is there primarily to keep our species alive. Which seems almost moot in today's world.

We recognize that people inherently have romantic and sexual desires, but does this always have to culminate in marriage or a similar long-term, monogamous relationship? Now before I get lambasted by my conservative friends, I'm not at all advocating anything radical. I've followed an incredibly traditional marital role in my own life. But it's valid to ask yourself if finding a lifelong mate is a priority for you, or is this expected drive merely a roadblock to other aspirations you authentically desire right now? There have been

great people of history who have found success and fulfillment in devotion to their work, and who didn't feel required
to follow the path of having a lifelong romantic union with
someone, any more than I felt I needed to attend college.
Can we question the norms here? Is marriage and perma-
nent *eros* love your priority? Are you unfulfilled without it?
Is time ticking and you may lose your shot? I challenge you
to consider what you really want versus what cultural norms,
expectations, and pressures you've thoughtlessly accepted. If
it *is* a key driver, fine. I'm just asking you to question it, as an
unquestioned expectation can take you down a very different life path than what you authentically desire.

Marital Relationships

Marriage is of course a subset of romantic relationships as
just covered, but I call it out specifically because it's one of
the greatest expectations of our culture, and I simply ask
if it should be your expectation. Now, or ever. I grew up in
the Bible Belt, where you go to church, you go to school,
you go to college, and then you get a job, get married, and
have kids. This is comparable to our daily requirement to
eat, drink, sleep, and breathe in order to exist. If it were not
a patent cultural expectation, is it what everyone would do?
Let me again stress that I am not necessarily advocating
or condoning anything outside of marriage and monogamy, but I am simply asking you to pose the question to
yourself of whether this kind of relationship is a drive you
authentically have or want, or are you simply kowtowing
to the pressure perfectly articulated by the father's plea in
My Big Fat Greek Wedding, "You so old. Get married. Make
babies." Is marriage and full-on life partnership what you
really desire? Is the idea of being devoted to your purpose/
calling/work so bad, especially when you can have a bevy

of deep relationships outside of romance and marriage? Are sexual relationships a requirement for life fulfillment? Being an athlete is a primary and vital aspect of my life fulfillment, but if you don't live the life of an athlete, are you missing out?

Parental Relationships

Like marriage, this is another culturally expected rite of passage, as ingrained in our society as wearing clothes in public. It's just what you do! I have nine children and have profound gratitude for the wealth of experience and massive fulfillment that fatherhood has provided me. Being a parent is now part of my DNA, and I could not give it more honor. That said, I also don't view it as a requirement for a full and glorious life. We're supposed to advocate and uphold everything we do, and I've done this with parenting and big families. I don't anymore. While I wouldn't trade my reality for anything, I greatly question people's desire to have kids and, even more, a lot of them. I don't feel being a business owner is best for everyone. Likewise, I don't see being a parent as a great fit for everyone. Again, we are no longer under great pressure to populate the Earth. Having a child is the most difficult business to start, run, and succeed with, yet it's often embarked on like getting a puppy, even though the gravity and responsibility is . . . just a bit more.

My brother Jared, in his involvement with space exploration, is an advocate of the overview effect, which is a psychological shift in awareness and conceptualization of existence one has when viewing Earth from outer space. *Star Trek* celebrity William Shatner recently related his experience of actually going into space, and said it literally brought him to his knees. He and all astronauts wish it was something we could all experience, for the value it brought to them. And such is the case for many people experiencing paradigm shifts. Yet I won't likely ever go to space myself because I don't really have any drive to. I also have no desire to hike Mount Everest, even though people say it's a life-changing event. There are so many experiences of profound value, and we can't experience them all. I have dear friends who never had children, and while they recognize parenthood's importance, they chose other experiences. And while I have been busy living life as a father to a large family, I've missed out on a wealth of other experiences in the process. Being a parent is just this: an experience. The challenge I put to you is to pull parenthood out of the realm of cultural expectation and ask yourself if you have a legitimate drive to have children.

I will say this: Having a child is a gift, and it's also a job. Again, it's akin to saying you want to start a business and become self-employed. I wish people would look at it with such gravity and even more. I find people who give more thought to getting a tattoo than having a child in considering the possible ramifications to their life.

Is this a drive you truly have within you? For you and you alone? Or is it a roadblock to your drive to pursue other life experiences?

Familial Relationships

Back to *My Big Fat Greek Wedding*. Even in the (perhaps?) exaggerated family dysfunctions portrayed in this movie and many, many others, we nevertheless continue to retain a certain reverence for familial relationships. For the purposes of this discussion, I am referring specifically to immediate and extended family, made up of biological, adopted, or however the core family of your upbringing was brought together.

How would you characterize your overall family ties, especially early on? Tight-knit, important, and valuable? Or harmful or traumatic? We're also in a time where there is more and more ambivalence toward family, and I fear the belonging we inherently desire is deteriorating.

We see so many who treat most family engagements as obligations. How many times have you seen that classic Christmas tableau of walking into a family setting, toting luggage along with dour faces and hearts? When it comes to family involvement after adulthood, a common perception is that of obligation, the sense that grown children don't really want to be around their families of origin. There are, of course, many who had traumas within their family and have rejected them altogether, for better or worse. There has and continues to be pain and abuse, and that pain is acute. We also have what more and more seems rare, people who authentically enjoy their families and find great value, belonging, and fulfillment. I grew up with a biblical charge to "honor thy father and mother" that generally extended to grandparents, aunts and uncles, and so forth. But is it truly honoring to engage with bitterness and mere obligation?

The challenge for you is to get in touch with your own feelings about your family. How do those perspectives and emotions around your family impact your drive for other relationships? What I want to get at the heart of here is the extended family structure you have and if you are in agreement with it—remembering there is not a right or wrong answer. Do you want intimate involvement with your family? Is it even possible? This is an opportunity to come to grips with what is, and what you want and feel is possible, and to set aside any lingering resentments about the family situation that you were given, but, of course, never chose for yourself.

Friends

This is where you and many may find their most beneficial *family*. You can't choose your blood, but you can choose
your friends. Musical artist Ben Rector has a wonderful
song titled "Old Friends" that recalls the memories of childhood and shared context and reality. As the saying goes,
you can't make old friends. You may not have had such an
idyllic childhood, however, and we now find ourselves in a
time when people may have thousands of so-called *friends*
on social media but not one real friend they could call in
the middle of the night for help.

But what type of friendship fits you? Is it the backslap-
ping, beer, and bowling club buddies that gather each week
to hang out and have fun? Is it a heavily entrenched group
of oddball friends depicted in the foundational sitcoms of
our times? From *Cheers* to *Seinfeld* to *Friends* to *The Office*,
we glorify these crazy yet seemingly intimate groups. Or
are you more of a *Semper Fi* type or *Ya Ya Sisterhood*?
Do you enjoy having many friends to call on or only one
or two deep friendships? What flavor of friendship calls
to you?

Then, what is the friendship platform? Fun and camaraderie? Shared context of life? Iron sharpens iron? Someone
to confide in? We have so many cultural overlays of what
friendships should and might look like, and I'm here to tell
you there is no right or wrong type of friendship, only the
kind that brings you fulfillment. Yet I see so many attempt-
ing to build friendships that don't really fit their nature.

Lasting friendships come from unions that give both
parties energy and affirmation. But so often people try to
sustain relationships that do not in fact build them up, but
instead drag them down. Sometimes there are places for
these relationships, but they don't qualify as true, lifegiving
friendship with equal give-and-take.

Movies and TV have many depictions of friendships we can analyze, but the key is to find one that authentically fits you. It's of interest to note that very few if any of the friendships seen on sitcoms involve people with children, and in life we often see people fall away from invested friendships once they become parents and succumb to the strong pull to put all their energy into the family unit. I should know, as a father of more than a few kids. How do you find adequate time for a friend when you have a spouse/significant other and kids? Which brings up another important issue of shared friends with your mate. Should you have the same friends? Is it OK to have individual friends? This of course is not for me to answer but for you to consider and decide upon as you discover what you authentically want for your friendships.

Social Groups

There are beneficial social groups and gatherings that may not qualify as friendships per se, but are nevertheless important to consider in our discussion of friendships. In the business world we often talk about networking groups, and it seems Chambers of Commerce are still relatively lively. Today these often happen online, and there are flourishing affinity groups around everything from business to hobbies to shared experiences of life. Be it a church or a running group, we find much value from communing with those who have shared interests. In addition to relational value there is great opportunity value from being with likeminded people, and engaging with such social groups can greatly increase our chances at progress in the areas of life we desire.

And yet what social exposure will best suit you? Kids are generally required to attend traditional school, whether it's a good social fit for them or not. "Christians" are expected to attend church regardless of the general structure being a good fit for them. If you start a small business in your local town, the Chamber of Commerce and many of your fellow business owners will try to pull you in. I have many friends who attend and benefit from business-related social groups. I have friends who do poker nights together. I have friends who often attend extracurricular faith-based social events. I seldom attend any, for better or worse. Chitchat is excruciating for me—I have significant auditory processing issues, plus I have internal pressure to people-please, so social events take a real toll on me. Yet I realize the benefit and am very select in what I do. As of this writing I have two podcasting events and a 12-hour, four-man mountain bike team event on my horizon, but my primary social group is four guys who meet every Friday at the coffee shop. The question is, what's the benefit you hope to gain by engaging with social groups? What appeals to you? A big group? A small group? A group that gathers to commune and have fun? A group with specific focal points? What type of social group would enhance your drive in certain areas of your life?

Coworkers

Even if you work solo in the sanctity of your home, you are likely to engage with other people in order to fulfill your work. Some of you work with scores of people, face-to-face, every day. As with social groups, we seldom take into account what fits us as individuals, as we tend to look toward the bottom line when it comes to work. I've known many solopreneurs who created successful ventures only to abandon them in order to go back to more collaborative and social work environments. While on the other hand,

I've seen people hired for their skills yet placed into work environments that required a lot of human interaction, which wore on them mightily.

We are in an age where big corporations realize how much time people spend at work, so they attempt to insert a bit of fun into the work environment. Casual dress days, coffee bars, and foosball tables were the hip accoutrements of Silicon Valley lore. Yet you are you. What is the work-relationship environment that would help you flourish? What would support and encourage you? What would inspire you? What would give you room to get your best work created? Would it be collaboration? Solitude? Camaraderie? Frequent meetings and discussions? There is much attention to such issues, but mainly given in broad brushstrokes, which ultimately misses the needs of individuals, and often forgets the primary goal, which should be to increase work performance and life fulfillment.

I'll take this opportunity to share what I feel is an important but divisive issue—collaboration. Collaboration is touted as best and good and right and true, and granted, few people can accomplish their best work without the support of and involvement with others. Collaboration is traditionally billed as coming together as a group to work closely together, helping each other in all our tasks. One, big, happy, reliant family. But this one-dimensional view misses many people.

I read a magazine article about a business startup founder who admitted quite frankly that she didn't want help when it came to her specific duties. She got energy and joy from doing it on her own. Yet this did not negate collaboration from her point of view. Her team came together to discuss the needs of a project, then while some worked hand in hand, she took her responsibilities behind her office door and did them solo. She gained energy and fulfillment in the creation process to have autonomy in her specific work. Yet she viewed the overall project as highly collaborative. If more than one person is involved in a job, it's collaboration, even if some may get more energy from fulfilling their roles autonomously. Going back to Jonathan Fields's Sparketype profile (www.sparketype.com), you can get a good sense of the type of collaboration and work relationships likely to fit you.

TAKE ACTION

What expectations might actually be roadblocks to your authentic relational drive? Where do you feel you may be at risk? Now how can you adjust accordingly?

HOW YOU WANT TO HAVE RELATIONSHIPS—AND WITH WHOM

To reiterate if I haven't enough already: the relationships we pursue are seldom thought out and intentional, instead they come primarily from unquestioned expectations and happenstance exposure. In essence, we're driving blind. Relationship expectations are also rife with moral and ethical baggage. I will undoubtedly come under scrutiny in discerning what I am or am not promoting regarding specific relational constructs. Let me state clearly that my intention is simply to enhance our overall life fulfillment by calling us all to question the norms and truly ask ourselves what would ultimately fulfill us as individuals. What relationships and relational qualities truly drive us?

Let me also, however, offer compassion to anyone who decides to buck the cultural norms, as there is undoubtedly a cost. To remain single, for instance, will come with the weight of labels and judgment, just as much as gender orientation, and I don't brush it off lightly. Labels such as "an old maid" or "a noncommittal bachelor" will likely be thought of by some. But now is your chance to question your internal relational drive: not what is expected of you, but what you will be fulfilled by. The good news, as I've said before, is that you have a lot of choices. We get to make our own beautiful relational soup and sample from every area to find where we truly have drive. Maybe you won't attach to a significant other. Maybe you will or maybe you won't have kids. Maybe you'll find a way to invest in kids, but not your own. Maybe you'll devote yourself to your work and those you work with. There are few fulfilled people who don't have very key relationships in their lives, but how this looks and feels varies widely.

TAKE ACTION

What do you authentically want for yourself within relationships? Be bold and don't discount anything.

WHAT MOTIVATES YOUR RELATIONSHIPS

While I appreciate the overall concept of committing to values and entrepreneurship, the movie *Jerry Maguire* contains one of the most damaging portrayals of relationships I've seen in the famously sappy "You complete me" scene.

A classic depiction of how incomplete we are deemed without the culturally expected relational wrappings, it assumes that anyone who is single is not whole, and I feel that's why we habitually seek to attach ourselves to people to fill our voids. Voids they can't fill. This is the setup for codependent and dysfunctional relationships.

The primary problem with relational motives and drive has to do with a massive dichotomy. The core motive of our entire lives is relationship with other humans. This is where we find our greatest purpose. Yet a core strength of our humanity is to be healthy and whole in and of ourselves. Most relational depictions fall too far on one side or the other. Hollywood produces glorifications of either grossly dysfunctional and dependent cravings for relationships or the lone-wolf machismo of someone who doesn't need anyone. Both are relatively psychotic and poison our views on what drives our relationships.

So, do we need someone to complete us or not? Going back to my discussion on roadblocks earlier in the chapter, we can ask this question regarding all relational constructs. Do we need to marry to be complete? Do we need to have children to be complete? What person(s) do we need in our life in order to be complete? Or maybe we're looking at it all wrong.

Some of my dearest friends are Scott and Hermine Stearman. Scott is a renowned sculptor whose life-size bronze masterpieces can be found at many military and faith-based institutions around America. Hermine was successful in the corporate world and then started a successful counseling practice. They never had children. Are they incomplete as people? Not whole? Or is this simply an aspect of life's experiences they did not partake of? They became godparents to my nine children and experience much of the glory of parenting but not the depth of birth and raising a child day in and day out. If we look at the entire possible experiences of life as a pie, this is a piece they did not fully take part in. But I would say they were not at all incomplete by not having children—they simply did not completely take part in all of life's experiences. And none of us can. It's impossible. While I was being a harried parent to so many kids, they were experiencing grand aspects of life I didn't have as much access or availability to. They traveled, built homes, and invested in so many other people. They benefited from so much *being* while I was so consumed with doing. Today I lean on them for imparting wisdom they accumulated in those special areas, just as I do with so many other people who have invested in life experiences I have not.

This concept of needing to be completed by another is what take us off course and causes the relational strife we as humans bear to be one of our greatest burdens. The glory lies in being as whole and complete as possible in and of ourselves, and coming to relationships to expand our life experience, depth, and wonder.

Now contrast this with the lone-wolf perspective. Number one, notice the movies never depict this person as being particularly happy and fulfilled, and second, in the end they almost always end up aligning with a romantic interest because that's the story we like most. I can simply say I've never encountered anyone of value to the world who didn't have a devotion to core relationships in their lives. I've never met a happy and enjoyable lone wolf, and whether we look at literal wolves and other animals or humans, we can deem it a myth. Enough said.

In the roadblock discussion, I stated that the first goal is to be whole and fulfilled in and of yourself. To be complete, contrary to the errant *Jerry Maguire* portrayal. Then pursue relationships from a desire for life experience and completion of the slices of life-pie you desire. If you desire romantic, *eros* love, why? What is your desire and goal? Do you want to take it further beyond romance and into long-term commitment and devotion? Why? What does it look like to you? Do you want to add on the love of parenting? Why?

In Chapter 3 I provided a list of negative feelings and descriptors, and it may be useful to revisit those and evaluate your current and past relationships for why you pursued them, and from there, try to uncover the needy reasons you may have had. Then, of course, consider how you want to positively and healthily revise current relationships and pursue new ones.

TAKE ACTION

What is motivating what you want for your relationships? What emotions do you feel? What circumstances are part of your why? In the relationships you have now, are you seeking to fill needs that are unfair and unhealthy? These are big questions that will likely take more digging into.

SEE YOURSELF THERE

If I had to guess the most popular tabloid content, judging by the covers I see while at the grocery checkout, it would be personal breakdowns and relational drama from celebrity couples. I make efforts to shield myself from bubble gum media, yet I still have awareness of the shenanigans of Ben and Jennifer, Kim and Kanye, and Beyoncé and Jay-Z. Unfortunately, I don't think these exaggerated (or not) depictions are benign, and they infiltrate our visions of what we do and don't want in relationships. Even the fairy tale Disney classics of our childhood seem to hold a fairly profound nucleus of influence toward our romantic relationships.

We often glamorize relationships, whether it's with romantic partners, our children, or coworkers, and don't fully consider what it would be like to live in that relationship in the real world. It is a powerful exercise to go back up to the relational categories listed in the "Roadblocks to Avoid" section, list out what you think you want, ask yourself why, make sure you are in agreement, then . . . envision it. Can you see yourself there?

Can you see yourself in a romantic relationship like the one you feel you want? A long-term committed union? How would it look and feel once the giddiness is hopefully still part of the relationship, but not all of it? Can you see yourself as a parent? What kind of parent? Do you envision yourself as a parent to a toddler or teenager? Can you see yourself learning to be the parent you would want to become? What kinds of friends do you want to have, and are you making strides to forge connections?

Next, I want you to really consider your role in relationships, as you will in fact embrace a certain role, and your chances of achieving the relational utopia you'd like has a far greater chance if you do just this—envision your role. You will be a character in the play of your relationships, and if you choose your character beforehand, you'll be headed toward an Oscar-worthy performance. You will play a role not only in and for your own life, but one that will vastly influence the butterfly effect of everyone you have a relationship with. What role will you play, and can you see yourself there?

You want to pursue the primary roles that truly drive you. Are you more the giver? The provider? The guide? How about the comforter or nurturer? Do you tend toward one way now, and are you at peace with it? Or if you are not and want to be, can you see yourself there? No one ever sets out to be the needy one or the villain or the antagonist, but they fall into this when they don't do the work we are engaging with right now.

YOUR RELATIONSHIP ZONE

If you want to take up running, it's easy to join a running group. Want to do art? It's easy to find an art club. But if you want to be a great spouse, partner, parent, coworker, or aunt, there's not a readily accessible group where you can simply enroll. Real knowledge and guidance for healthy and whole relationships can be elusive, and we tend to be overly influenced by the relationships we have been exposed to but did not choose.

As we've covered previously, your first place to look for good relationships is in the mirror, and in your past. Your greatest, most positive and influencing relational zone is getting to be aware of yourself—your relationship with yourself and others. Taking responsibility for how it has been and, more importantly, how you want it to be. And here's the thing about self-awareness. You can't do it by yourself. Take the old saying "You can't see the forest for the trees." When it comes to ourselves, we are the trees. We are fairly incapable of achieving viable self-awareness in a vacuum. In business branding terms, the reality is we can't say what our brand is. We try to influence it, but at the end of the day, it's our customers and audience who say what our brand truly is. In seeking self-awareness, we will evaluate ourselves by our intent, while others will judge us by their experience of us. Granted, their experience is diluted by their bias, thus you may want to get feedback on who and how you are by someone who is unbiased, and with expertise in the field. Yes, I mean a counselor or a therapist.

Professional ballplayers on a team are provided with the very best coaches and trainers. It's part of the team and the contract. Yet most additionally employ personal trainers on their own time to finely hone their specific skills and needs. And here we are, trying to excel as human beings, and we only seek expert trainers when we are in dire straits. Is this crazy, or is it just me? In truth, it has been me too. Just ask my therapist.

Your first relational zone is with yourself, and I'd advocate getting someone to help you see yourself.

But you can look at relationships of all varieties and seek ways to gain exposure. When you see a committed couple together, seek to be in their company and try to learn from what you see. Or be bold enough to simply ask them. How did they get to the healthy state you perceive them as achieving? Chances are, they will be honored you asked, and you may hear of significant trials they went through to arrive at the health they have today, which will give you perspective. It's likely you'll get some nuggets of wisdom you can use.

Same with parenting. In my own experience, I was so privileged to have some mentors and resources that were foundational, and they helped my wife and me parent with at least a modicum of success. We have dramatic relational resources to glean from, yet we are more prone to seek out guidance on work, finances, or health than on relationships. It reminds me of a meme on Reddit asking, "If someone from the 1950s suddenly appeared today, what would be the most difficult thing to explain to them about life today?" The anonymous answer, "I possess a device, in my pocket, capable of accessing the entirety of information known to man. I use it to look at pictures of cats and get into arguments with strangers."

CHAPTER SUMMARY

▶ **Case for Relationships:** When it comes down to it, life can lack value or purpose outside of relationships. Yet we seldom think through what kinds of relationships we want, and just accept the cultural norms. This is your chance to truly consider what relationships you authentically want.

▶ **What Is Inherent:** You inherit more than just your eye or hair color from your parents and grandparents. Understanding familial relationship patterns can help you come to terms with some of your own relational inclinations, so you can adjust accordingly.

▶ **What You've Been Exposed To:** How your parents or primary caregivers approached relationships had a tremendous influence, causing you to either mirror or rebel against what was demonstrated to you in your childhood. Consider how that environment may have influenced your current relationships.

▶ **Roadblocks to Avoid:** How have cultural norms dictated what relationships we should have, and how they should look? What have you agreed with? What have you blindly accepted?

▶ **What You Authentically Want:** Step back from the expectations. There are likely relationships you are in that are not fitting, and perhaps some fitting ones you haven't found just yet. It's now time to ask what you authentically want for yourself relationally, and what truly fits you.

▶ **What Motivates You:** This may take some real work to get to the root of what truly motivates your relationships. Or lack thereof. Look for voids, codependencies, or dysfunction. Are there any relationships you are using as a crutch? Think of how your relationships can expand, not constrict, your life.

▶ **See Yourself There:** Picture yourself in the relationships you want. Consider how you want to feel and what your role would be. Relationships don't just happen, they are created.

▶ **Your Relationship Zone:** Find people who have the relationships you desire. Rub shoulders with them and learn from them.

CHAPTER 5

What Drives Your Body

You Are How You Look and Feel

Lori Harder began life as an overweight kid in an overweight family where the primary social activity was plopping down on the couch, watching TV, and eating snacks. Lori's family followed a strict religion and remained very isolated, leaving her with very little exposure beyond the walls of her home and the unhealthy environment. While more children today are overweight and childhood obesity is unfortunately normalized, back then being a "fat kid" was a calling card for bullying, and Lori found herself on the receiving end to a tragic degree. One day, however, she came upon her sister working out to a VHS tape, and it introduced a new idea into her life. Lori began joining her sister in the workouts. Initially her physical appearance didn't change because of her consistently poor eating habits, but she realized the workouts caused her to feel better and her constant anxiety abated following the sessions. She thought more clearly and slept better.

Not long after, Lori paid a rare visit to a new friend's home and witnessed a very different family dynamic. They didn't live in front of the TV, and junk food was not the primary staple. They engaged in activities beyond the couch and a bag of tempting chips. Lori noticed they weren't as preoccupied with food and mere entertainment, because they were busy with other, more enjoyable endeavors. This opened up Lori's world even more.

Then one fateful day she stumbled upon a fitness competition on TV and recalls, "The strong, beautiful women displayed superhero-like acts on stage. My world screeched to a halt. I wanted to be just like these women, and I wanted to provoke powerful, positive feelings for others just like these women were doing for me. As I shifted my focus to fitness, not only did I improve my body, but I started to feel amazing. Feeling strong in my body put me in control and lit a fire inside my soul that got me thinking about new possibilities for my life. I wanted to show others that they too had the power to change, so I dedicated the next two decades of my life to educating myself on food and fitness."

Lori ultimately pursued a career as a fitness competitor and model, gracing the covers of multiple fitness magazines, but today she is fully devoted to leading and influencing other women to better, healthier, and happier versions of themselves as an author, speaker, and podcaster. On one of my podcast episodes, Lori said there was always a burning desire in her to do more than just better her own life. She wanted to help others to find the freedom and joy she experienced, as she realized most everyone lives with limiting perspectives, which they carry forward into their adult lives.

Lori's story is similar to Ben Hardy's, in that there was no single, cataclysmic event that triggered her drive and ensuing transformation. Just a seed of discomfort and dissatisfaction, met with little fertilizations of possibility. And slowly her drive grew and revealed itself and propelled her forward into a radical life change. Look beyond Lori's fitness competitions and modeling and pay attention to her childhood experience of feeling better, sleeping better, managing her anxiety, and leaving behind the bullying aimed at her obese physique and insecure self-image.

In our affluent society with more technology, knowledge, and convenience than ever before, you'd think we'd have every reason to be healthier and happier than ever, yet the stats show we are in fact sicker and sadder than ever. The US Centers for Disease Control cites over a quarter (27.2 percent) of US adults have multiple chronic conditions, up from 21.8 percent in 2001. I've deeply pondered the root issues of why we've lost our way. My finding is that as we've lost touch with the deeper appetites of our core values and purpose, we medicate by constantly feeding ourselves with the next dopamine hit of food and entertainment, and it's taking its toll with unprecedented speed. In America we spend more money on "healthcare" than anything else. Most of it goes to trying to fix problems we are causing by sedentary lifestyles, unhealthy food, and lack of purpose. One of our fastest growing areas of illness is now called "diseases of despair," derived from conditions people experience due to a sense that their long-term social and economic outlook is bleak. Nutritionally, economically, and opportunistically, we are massively overfed and yet undernourished.

I feel fairly confident in claiming that everyone wants to look and feel great, as I've not yet met anyone who boldly states otherwise. Though many will admit to not *wanting* to do what it takes to look and feel great, even as they concede it's possible. So let me pose a question: What is the measuring stick for your life fulfillment? Only you can say. In the previous chapter I touched on the importance of your relationship with yourself, which is the foundation of all your relationships. A significant part of this relationship with yourself is how you literally feel—or your general state of wellness. And the second is how you *feel* about how you look.

To illustrate this further, I'll ask you to picture a chart with two columns: A, "Problems/Pathologies" and B, "Performance." Under column A, list out the aches, pains, and inabilities you are OK with. Under column B, list out what you want to be physically capable of. Many people are clear about what they do and don't want in a job, house, car, or even a relationship. But ask them what they do and don't want regarding their body, and they draw a blank. Most will vaguely recite they just want to lose weight and feel better. But think about it: What pathologies are you in agreement with? Think of it like a menu list. Would you go along and check things off, thinking . . . *Yeah, I'm OK not being able to be very physically active anymore. My knees and back ache, but . . . OK by me. And migraines . . . it's only once or twice a week. I'm cool with that. Some brain fog . . . sure. As long as I can manage to keep my job. High blood pressure? No biggie, they've got meds for that. Crippling PMS? Hey, just comes with being a woman. Achy knees and I can't really take the stairs anymore . . . that's what elevators are for, right?* We can go on and on, but regarding the problems with your body, what are you OK with? Why do we have lower expectations for the "vehicle" of our body, and why do we generally tend to it with less consistent care and maintenance?

Column B of my chart is Performance. Very few people other than the culturally labeled "health and fitness nuts" consider this. But what do you want for your physical performance? Anything other than being able to get out of bed and to your desk?

In June 2022, 83-year-old Kenichi Horie made headlines for sailing solo across the Pacific Ocean and setting a world record for being the oldest person to do so. This repeats a feat Kenichi accomplished 60 years ago at age 23. Most will write him off as an anomaly and say it's just genetics and luck of the draw. Similarly, Irving Gordon has a world record for his 1966 Volvo P1800S having over three million miles on it. Another anomaly? Of course not. You'd expect to hear exactly what is true, that Irving took great care of that vehicle, changing the oil, driving it moderately, and tending to its upkeep. But we don't give Kenichi and other older people credit when they maintain their physical and mental capacities late into life. We can't live forever. But most of the decline in aging is not a chronological problem but a wear-and-tear problem. In this way, human bodies and cars are very similar.

Let me clue you into a massively deceptive myth: Your mind does not function separately from your body. If you are walking slower up the stairs, your mind is moving slower too. We'll cover this more in the next chapter. But if you have body aches and pains, these are not isolated issues but little warning lights of an overall system malfunction. Our body is built for survival and will do its best, but as our health declines the telltale signs will manifest in all varieties of ways depending on our physical makeup. Beneath each little (or big) manifestation is a body in crisis.

TAKE ACTION

How do you see yourself? Regarding your physical body, what are you most proud of? What are you not proud of? Are there pathologies or maladies you have just chalked up to normal aging? What physical performance do you desire for yourself now? In 5 years? In 20 years?

HOW YOUR GENETICS LOOK AND FEEL

To reference geneticist Francis Collins and his quote again, "Genetics loads the gun and environment pulls the trigger." Meaning we are all born with genetic predispositions and propensities. But by and large, it is our chosen lifestyle that causes the manifestation, or not, of most of our problems.

I have seven biological kids. Same mom and dad. My son Ian seems to have been so influenced by his Scottish name he actually developed the Scots fair skin. He starkly stands out among my other kids as uber white. I've no idea where this came from—I guess it was just his genetic luck of the draw. He can be out in the sun like the rest of us and burn like mad, and therefore has a higher risk of ending up with skin cancer later in life. But he works with this genetic propensity, not against it. He avoids the direct, hot sun. When swimming, he'll often have a shirt on. And a hat. And extra sunscreen. This is while his parents and siblings frolic around relatively free from a severe sunburn threat. He is actively working to not pull the trigger of his genetically loaded complexion propensity. He can claim it's unfair and rebel by being out in the sun and burning himself silly, or he can deal with it.

Two of my kids are adopted and are 100 percent Native American. Their genetic propensity for diabetes is off the charts. We go to great lengths to limit sugar and empty carbs and keep that loaded gun from being triggered. It's so unfortunate for them. It's not fair, and it's not their fault. But living to their fullest capacity is now much under their control.

We went through a few years of hosting elite runners in the Army's World Class Athlete Program at our home for high altitude training. Our home sits at 9,200 feet above sea level. The runners would come spend the night, then do a

20-mile run the next day. Spend the night again, then go down to Colorado Springs at only 6,200 feet and do a speed workout with more oxygen available. The majority of the runners were from Kenya. In asking about their lifestyle, a couple shared the same story. "We lived away from town, so in the morning we would run two to three miles to school." I asked, "Did you have recess? And if so, what did you do?" They responded, "We'd run around, and play soccer." "Oh wow, more running," I replied. To which one piped in with, "Well, then the school didn't provide lunch, so we'd run home for that, then back to school. And after school, run back home." Then they added on later, "We didn't have shoes, so we did it barefoot." This was their life. This was their parents' lives and their parents before them. Is it a wonder Kenyans win more running medals than anyone? They have generations of body adaption to the long-term elevated heart rate and pounding of their feet. This, combined with a continued lifestyle to pull the trigger of their loaded gun, helps make them faster than a bullet.

We see this happen with diet as well. When you take a culture that eats a predominant diet, you generally find people from the culture function better on this same diet long-term. If you are from Greenland where mattak is popular, which is whale skin and fat (blubber), often eaten raw, you'll likely perform well on skin and fat. If you're from Bangladesh, the least meat-consuming country in the world, you may do very poorly trying to perform well on mattak.

My intention is not to present an academic exploration into genetics, and I am admittedly oversimplifying it. I'm highly sensitive to those who may have significant genetic deficits, but at the end of the day we either accept our genes and adjust our lifestyle accordingly, or we submit to being a victim of them and let them handicap us. You have the opportunity and responsibility of doing the research and finding out what all you have to work with. The good and bad ingredients that make up your physiological predispositions. Strengths and weaknesses. Then leveraging and bending to accommodate them to be at your best. Overall I find far too many people lamenting their poor lot in life, and fewer folks putting on their big girl or big boy pants and taking responsibility to do the best with what they have. Thank goodness you are the latter, or you wouldn't be reading this.

There is great benefit in understanding your family history of health issues. There are many advanced diagnostic and genetic tests you can utilize to discover as much as possible about your natural biological strengths and weaknesses so you can, again, adjust and advocate for yourself. But please understand, as to Francis Collins's statement, the greatest threat to your genetic weaknesses is not being born with them, but feeding them with your lifestyle.

TAKE ACTION

What are the genetic realities or propensities you see in your biological family's past? How did they eat? How did they exercise and move? What ailments were common?

HOW YOUR ENVIRONMENT LOOKS AND FEELS

I'll never forget a moment I had in a physical therapist's office back in my pro cycling days. While I was getting treated for some wreck-induced leg injury, a middle-aged woman and her mother came in. As the doctor was asking questions about the middle-aged woman's back problems, she said, "Oh, my mom has this same problem, all my sisters do; it just runs in the family." And the doctor retorted, rather bluntly, "No. From what I gather, you have practiced the same poor posture as your mother, sitting beside you. You've eaten the same poor diet, and you've all been very sedentary." An old joke cites a guy at a doctor's appointment saying, "You see, doc, obesity runs in my family." To which the doctor replies, "No, the problem is *nobody* runs in your family." It may seem harsh and you may feel it's unfair, but being involved in the health, wellness, and medical community and industry as much as I have, this truth plays out far more than mere genetic blame. We can certainly ask if any malady is primarily a genetic malfunction or a lifestyle malfunction. You'll serve yourself best to adopt the latter, which gives you agency and hope.

My friend Jennifer Poole was talking about her joy in running, and I asked where it came from. "I come from a running family," she replied. Her statement really hit me as I thought about the type of environment I wanted to foster with my children. I wanted to be a "running family," and to date, every one of our kids has run cross-country in school. And even though none of them found a great love for running itself, they all appreciated the physical and social benefits, and it helped implant physical fitness into their lives.

The workplace can also be an incredibly influential place for our health and wellness. One of my favorite examples of this comes from a member of a self-employment community I ran who wanted to get into shape. To start his journey, he preregistered for a 5k run a few months down the road and even registered for an out-of-town marathon a year away—buying the plane tickets and booking the hotel as well. His motivation there alone was impressive, but what happened next is what's most interesting to me. At his place of employment, he started going for a walk during his lunch break. Thankfully, instead of receiving criticism, he was encouraged. Soon someone asked to join him. It didn't take long before he had a small group going on walks with him, and that later turned into jogging.

This is a beautiful example of such a seemingly little thing sparking a positive health movement. If more people spawned a lunchtime walking club, I think we'd see vast improvements in work and lives. The benefits of healthy activities in the workplace have a ripple effect far beyond the mere physical benefit to muscles and lungs. You get happier, more productive people.

Looking at your own family and upbringing, how was health and wellness viewed? Let's first look at exercise and movement. Most kids, at least before personal computers became ubiquitous, had very active childhoods. But even so, if their parents are not active, the kids will generally follow their example. Once we graduate from school and mandatory recess, most people settle into a sedentary life-style. Even sports is not a great predictor of a future active lifestyle, as once the competition is over, again, most will stop consistent movement.

Don't miss the relevance of the word I just used: *movement*. This is the point. Our ancestors had no use for the word *exercise*, as life was exercise. To survive, you had to move. This was a fact of life until a few generations ago. It's only in recent times where we don't have to move in order to exist. It's not just the advent of desk jobs; even much of the manual labor industry has automated tasks so a machine does more of the effort than the physical body. We seldom have reason to increase our heart rate or stress our muscles. And without some physical stress, muscles atrophy. Without movement as a necessity, we must artificially manufacture movement, which we call exercise. And most people view it as a necessary evil, if they view it at all.

This is then where you want to examine how movement and exercise was exemplified in your upbringing—it may have been absent. Your caregivers went to work, came home, plopped down at the table for dinner or maybe directly to the couch for the evening, then to bed. Repeat. Maybe there was some exercise. Possibly as a necessary evil. A begrudging activity in an effort to keep up appearances or follow the doctor's guidance to keep the old ticker going.

If you are fortunate, there was a healthy example of exercise and movement, hopefully in the form of play. The family engaged in physical activity together, and Mom played tennis and Dad went out for pickup games of basketball with the guys. Summers were at the ocean or lake or mountains, swimming, exploring, and exhausting yourself. Maybe you played sports and your caregivers did more than come to the games but they practiced with you as well. And from all of this you developed a healthy and joyful relationship with physical activity and movement and continued on with it into your adult life. The power, of course, is in considering the example you were given and responding to it. If you were fortunate, be grateful and continue. If you grew up in a sedentary, lethargic family like Lori Harder did, then see it clearly and admit, "That is not a healthy example and something I want to emulate," and instead commit to a new paradigm. You will view exercise and movement as play and with gratitude and excitement for what it adds to your life and start a new legacy of joy in play and movement.

Food and nutrition are very similar. For some it was a nonissue—you just ate what was put in front of you with no thought. Eating was simply like throwing wood in a stove to burn, and it didn't matter what type of food it was, so it might as well be the easy, exaggerated tastes of processed foods high in salt and sugar. Or maybe there were attempts at healthy eating? Maybe your parents got on "kicks" of trying to eat more veggies and less junk food. Or maybe they yo-yo dieted? If you are fortunate, food was a joy. A cornucopia of not only eating whole food, but reveling in the environment of harvesting, cooking, breaking bread, and rejoicing.

TAKE ACTION

How was movement and exercise perceived in your family? Was it considered a drudgery or something fun and valuable? Was it considered at all? How has this influenced you? Even if you currently engage in exercise, how do you really feel about it? Is it a necessary evil or a joyful pastime? How about your beliefs regarding food and nutrition? Was nutrition even a topic of discussion in your house? Was there abuse and control around food? Were you shamed? And ultimately, how do you feel about healthy eating today?

ROADBLOCKS TO AVOID

If you read a lot of self-help and fitness books, you might come to the conclusion that discipline and willpower are what make someone a consistent exerciser and partaker of good nutrition. But you'd be mistaken. What we find lending to the greatest success is simply the attitude one has toward these topics, as well as their environment. The people who exercise the most and eat the best, long term, are those who attribute good feelings about them and who surround themselves with like-minded people. If you feel supported by those around you in reaching healthy goals, very little discipline or willpower is really needed.

In my friend Dr. Randy James's practice, he finds most patients willing and often eager to engage in the life-changing alterations he prescribes for them. Left to themselves they would happily go to bed earlier, get up earlier, exercise, buy and prepare healthy meals, meditate, and more. But here's the rub. They are not left to themselves. They have the programming from their past and the people of their present to contend with.

As we've covered in the two previous sections on genetics and environment, most of us end up in adulthood with specific feelings toward health and wellness, and the positive or negative perspectives will either support or sabotage our efforts. In America we have a predominant assumption that healthy food is all about one word—deprivation. The cultural attitude toward healthy eating is primarily focused on what you *can't* eat.

I'll never forget a lady from a church we attended in our small mountain town. A lady in very poor health. She and her husband were both ravaged by a lifetime of unhealthy living. As she was struggling to even walk in the grocery store, toting her oxygen tank while she picked out the worst of processed foods from the middle aisle, a friend recommended maybe she go see Dr. James, who had helped so many people find a new lease on life. The lady responded (as it was later recounted to me), "Go to Dr. James? No thanks, he'll make me throw out everything in my pantry and force me to eat all that healthy stuff."

If your attitude about healthy eating is one of deprivation and the end of all joy, your chances at long-term consumption of nutritious, life-giving food is doomed. If you relate to this feeling, you are in good company. Don't berate yourself. But now you know the work you must do. To do justice to the concept of nutrition is a book or more in itself, and I won't attempt to adequately address it here. I'll highly recommend Michael Pollan's book *Food Rules*, which is a fun 30-minute read. If you pay attention, it will turn your dietary perspective upside down with absolutely practical and immediately actionable advice, such as Rule 20: "It's not food if it arrived through the window of your car."

But if I could gift you with a winning perspective, one I'll actually claim I originated, it's this: we are, and will always be, creatures of our appetites. If your goal is to squelch your appetite, you will fail. You must feed your appetite if you want a joyful and sustainable life. The key is to simply *elevate* your appetite. And practice some delaying tactics.

I read a quote somewhere saying, and I paraphrase, "The key to healthy eating is not to deprive, but delay." I love it. I love imbibing. I love celebrating. I love feasting. Life is far too short to deprive myself of it. But I will, for my overall wellness and ultimate joy, delay it. And in the delay, the partaking is so much sweeter. Do you love a bag of chips and a movie? Great! Enjoy it once a week. Twice if you must. Just not nightly. Do you adore chocolate, as I do? Great. Instead of a bag (or four!) of M&Ms or high sugar chocolate, I follow most lunches and dinner with a small handful of dark chocolate almonds I've come to like far more than the processed, diabetes-inducing distant cousins.

Find your vices and dietary loves and start moving them to healthier forms. Try real, homemade options. Or substitutes. But hold on, if that thought is also detestable and there is just no way you're substituting some veggie chip for your beloved Doritos or Pringles, then don't. But do it less frequently. Actually, even with the veggie chip, still, let it be less frequent. Many "healthy alternatives" may be healthier than the cultural norm, but still fall far short of actually being healthy. They are lesser evils at best.

I went through a time of substituting all my vices with healthier options. But I admit, if I'm going to have pie or cheesecake, I'm not scrimping. I'm delaying, then fully partaking. Find your own secret sauce for sustaining these new habits, but know that focusing on deprivation is not tenable.

As deprivation is the death knell of healthy eating, dread is the killer of sustainable exercise and movement. If your New Year's resolution is to run every day while you tell everyone you hate running, you'll likely be done in less than 30 days. Possibly the best counsel I've ever heard on this subject I again attribute to Dr. Randy James. When asked by his patients what is the best exercise, he retorts with, "Whichever one you'll do." Erase the beliefs about fit people being so disciplined and full of willpower. I get that all the time when people hear about my daily trail runs and mountain bike rides. And it couldn't be further from the truth. I'm not disciplined, I'm just playing! It's like recess to head out into the woods and get lost on a trail. I have friends who feel the same about playing soccer, tennis, or ultimate frisbee; skiing; swimming; or taking a Zumba class.

Here is another oddity. We've gotten to a point where we delegate all our household physical tasks and then go to the gym to perform completely artificial exercises. Try washing your car yourself for some movement instead of driving it through the car wash. Mow your own yard with a regular push mower. Take up gardening instead of signing up for yoga class. Repaint that room or your house yourself. Remember, exercise is a substitute for the normal movement we no longer require to survive.

TAKE ACTION

When you think of healthy eating, how do you feel about it? What emotions come up? "Depriving" is a death knell you must vanquish. And the same with exercise. If the very thought is drudgery, you are doomed. What movement would you enjoy? What physical play could you engage with? Remember Dr James's counsel: the best exercise is whatever one you'll consistently do!

The second and possibly most dangerous roadblock to your pursuit of health and wellness is simply the people and environment you surround yourself with. Many well-meaning and inspired individuals cave in under the pressure of family, friends, or coworkers and the norm of the environment. We long to belong. This is the inspiration behind Dan Buettner's *Blue Zones* books. The healthiest and happiest people in the world live in communities where living out the attributes of health and wellness are the norm, so they don't even have to try. Everyone is walking and moving as part of their day and eating the local fare of whole and natural foods. This is why communities such as Weight Watchers, Curves, Peloton, and CrossFit have had such success—they immerse you in a culture of like-minded people. Alcoholics Anonymous is arguably the most successful life-change organization ever due to the "Blue Zone" of support and accountability it creates.

When you decide to eat healthy and exercise and veer from the cultural norm, it's uncomfortable. And we don't like discomfort, especially socially. If your family is eating fast-food meals for dinner and you're trying to eat sardines and broccoli, you're at a disadvantage. Much more so if you are chided or flat-out criticized for it by your family or friends. Coworkers can be just as bad. Nobody wants to be the person who declines the office donuts or pizza or birthday celebration cake. I saw this play out starkly in my own home. I live in a Blue Zone. I share offices with people who routinely whip out leftovers from last night's dinner of veggies and whole foods for lunch. Or if one is fasting the others are likely to join in. The same goes for our closest family friends. So my kids grew up not knowing much else. Most have never eaten fast food, and we've had fun with the younger ones asking questions as they get older, such as, "Daddy, what's a Pop-Tart?"

We homeschooled a lot, but even with the younger kids in private and public schools, they were fine taking lunches of veggies and hummus and fish. Then, middle school happened. What I found was that the kids were generally not eating lunch. They cared about their health enough not to partake of the school fare of chicken nuggets and pizza, but they didn't want to be so weird as to pull out a home lunch of "healthy food." So they just didn't eat. They'd have breakfast, then wait till they got home to eat something worthwhile. This social pressure is where many of us find ourselves.

To cite Ben Hardy again, in his book *Willpower Doesn't Work*, he makes a case for our willpower being finite and ultimately failing us, and the key to success is to craft our environment for success. Which for good dietary habits would mean not buying chips, ice cream, and other temptations to have lying around. It's easy to withstand temptation if the temptation is absent. But again, if your family is buying the stuff and your workplace has it around and your friends, family, and coworkers are habitually and socially dragging you to fast food and the bar, you are in for a struggle.

These are the roadblocks. How you deal with them is now your homework. You must figure out how to get a positive mindset toward healthy eating and exercise. You must figure out how to deal with the people surrounding you and the challenges of your environment. I will offer counsel to the latter. While you may not want to ditch your current family, friends, and coworkers, you will be foundationally well served to start spending time with a Blue Zone of your own. A community of like-minded people where your culturally abnormal ways are normal and encouraged. Even having one person as a partner in your corner is monumental.

HOW YOU WANT TO LOOK AND FEEL

You are now faced with deciding, likely for the first time, how you want to look and feel, for you and you alone. The question itself is incredibly paradoxical, as it's hard for us to separate how we look and feel from how it relates to others. After all, the main reason we wash ourselves, brush our teeth and hair, shave, put makeup on, dress, and tend to our weight is because of others. To help you answer this question, I'll guide you through a visualization:

Tomorrow you are going to wake up in another city. Maybe another country. You have a home and money in the bank. Access to meaningful work if you want it. But you get to show up however you want. A fresh start. Who and how do you want to be? For yourself. What makes you proud as you look in the mirror and, with that image, walk out into the world? Remember, you don't know anyone. There is no past history. No baggage. You are free. How would you like to show up?

How we look and feel does have a very realistic opportunity cost. People do judge a book by its cover. But for this exercise, try to cut those concerns out of the picture. Assume you can have the job of your dreams. You can have the guy or girl of your dreams who fawns over you no matter what. You get status, money, and love no matter what. Still, how would you choose to show up? If it didn't matter, would you choose to show up unshaven, unwashed, unkempt, and unfit? Would you truly be OK with this? I'm not fishing here but authentically trying to bring you to a place of personal ownership for how you look and feel.

The hard truth is we are and will be judged by how we look and feel, just as we judge others in the same way. I am very well aware of how I look and feel and how it benefits or penalizes me in the real world. I can't disassociate from it. Yet for my own happiness and sustainability, I try. I want to be who I am for me. For Kevin. I want to be the image I'm proud of for me. I want to show up in the world as the avatar I feel good about.

In my early adult years, I spent a couple of years working in the real estate industry. I always found it off-putting that the glamour shots of Realtors featured on the billboards and business cards were usually taken 10 years and 20 pounds ago. Now first off, that's bad business. Just like with personal ads, you don't want to oversell yourself only to have the person's first encounter with you be one of disappointment. But second and relevant to this topic is the question, if they use a past and primped picture as the image they put out to the world, then it would behoove them to really own that image and live up to it. If they don't do that, there seems to be a cognitive dissonance with their self-image.

Let's not forget the aspect of how we want to feel. I gave you my two columns of Pathologies and Performance previously. What physical performance do you want from yourself? What pathologies are you OK with? You can answer these questions for today and for your future, as what you are capable of today dictates your capability for your future. If you want to be an 83-year-old capable of self-piloting yourself on a sailboat across the Pacific like Kenichi Horie, remember he started as a 23-year-old who was capable of such a feat, and he never let himself decline from there. If you want to be the 83-year-old who is able to participate physically and cognitively with your family and friends, you are building the ability, or not, today. Physical ability only maintains through resistance. Without resistance you are feeding atrophy. You don't wake up shuffling along with a walker. You get there day by day with less resistance and less activity. It takes decades of habits to get your feet and mind to a shuffling status.

I see this play out in the workplace when people view their jobs and businesses only in regard to money and security, which harkens back to a scarcity mentality. When you merely do what's asked and don't risk trying new things, you'll find yourself surpassed by someone (or something like AI) who does it faster, cheaper, or better. Staying at the top requires proactively seeking resistance and strengthening.

Our culture often talks about life span—how long your heart keeps beating. We seldom address *health span*, which is how long we remain vital and able. Unlike animals, we have separated life span and health span and now accept a loss of health, wellness, and ability long before our life ends. Randy made the observation about the elk herds often found crossing my mountain property. He said he'd never seen one trailing the herd, hobbling along with a walker and an oxygen tank. They are going strong, right up to the end when they acutely become ill or injured and die quickly from natural causes or a predator. We as humans, however, let our ability fade and then linger for years.

TAKE ACTION

As difficult as it is to separate how we look from our relation to others, how do you want to look for you and you alone? What is your desired self-image? Your chosen avatar? And how do you want to feel? What capacity and capability do you want for yourself? What pathologies and performance do you desire?

WHAT MOTIVATES HOW YOU LOOK AND FEEL

This brings into the crosshairs our own self-interest. Our motive for how we look and feel is not a static topic. We do everything out of self-interest, in my experience and opinion, but there is a profound difference between self-interest we own for ourselves and self-interest we give others ownership of. Meaning, if I'm trying to look fit to attract a mate, am I exercising for them or for myself? If I'm sitting over here eating healthy, that doesn't make my prospective mate's life better. My exercising doesn't help their blood pressure or waist measurement. If I do the work to be fit and trim and someone is attracted to me, the benefit of my effort is all mine. I get a mate and all the benefits are for myself. In theory, if the prospective mate is not attracted to me, they will simply stroll on and find another mate. My efforts are for myself. I own them for me. Psychologically this is a primary dictate for your health and wellness success. And from a human relationship aspect, why would we let go of a key aspect of human attraction? I'd think anyone would appreciate their significant other looking good, feeling good, making money, enjoying life, and more.

We've all seen the person who is young, fit, and trim; finds a mate, and gets married. And then "lets themselves go," as we say. At some point down the line, let's say they get a divorce. What so often happens? They go get fit and trim again. It's a classic example of self-interest they gave ownership to someone else for. They are only doing it to achieve a goal and are not owning it for themselves. It's the same reason we see pro athletes at the pinnacle of physical performance, only to retire and fall into poor health. It's incredibly common. Without the end zone or net to strive for, they have no motive. Then there are the few who saw themselves as more than competitors on a team or in a race, but as true, lifelong athletes.

Notice that few overweight people claim they *authentically* want to lose weight. Likewise, few people discovering physical ailments claim they authentically want to recover and rehab. What do they say instead? "I should." This single word (the "s" word) conveys a complete lack of personal motive and ownership, and this is why we as a culture so often fail at maintaining our health and wellness. "Shoulds" don't sustain us. When it comes to your motives, I encourage you to abolish "I should" from your vocabulary. Leave it back in your childhood when you said, "I should clean my room," when you had no personal desire and it was simply a dependent responding to an authority. This is no way to live as an adult. The key to your drive is you being your own authority and nobody else.

Regarding health and wellness, let me give you some experiential evidence. If your main motivator for pursuing fitness is primarily to look good for other people, it won't stick. You may achieve your goal for a season, but it will invariably end. The people who sustainably stay looking good are primarily motivated by *how they feel and look for themselves*. Go back to Lori Harder's story as an obese kid. Her initial experience and motive for working out was simply feeling better, sleeping better, and having less anxiety. Those are things she owned for herself. It wasn't losing weight and attracting a boy. She benefited from that later, but it wasn't the instigator.

Let me stress this again: your motive for looking good must include *feeling* good, or it won't result in a sustaining drive for your life. How you look can be a great by-product, but shouldn't be the key driver. I've witnessed people make great gains in their health and biomarkers that will increase their mental capacity and add vibrant years to their lives, only to abandon it because they didn't make the weight loss or measurements they wanted. What a tragedy. I think the world health crisis would abate if we could turn all the motive from simply attracting a mate, to *being able to mate* in our eighties and nineties!

Using the car analogy again, we are all highly motivated to frequently change the oil in our automobiles. To get new tires and brakes. To replace a cracked windshield or misfiring engine. If we don't the problem will only get worse, until we can't drive the car. Changing the oil doesn't make the car drive better at that particular moment. Rather, it makes it drive better in 10 years. It's the same with our bodies. Eating good food, exercising, and taking our vitamins and supplements may not always result in us feeling better in the moment or the next day. But it's what will help us feel better next year. Next decade. This is a sustaining drive.

TAKE ACTION

When you think about how you want to look, what
is your motive? Is it a *should* you don't really feel for
yourself? How do you want to feel, and why? Do you
have thoughts and desires for your future self?

SEE YOURSELF THERE

We become what we expect. Pithy but oh so true. If you
truly desire to look and feel different, can you authentically
see yourself that way? You perceive yourself according to
what you believe to be true. This will require faith. Can
you really, in your mind's eye, see yourself looking and
feeling different? In the case of health and wellness and
how you look and feel, a relevant aspect of seeing yourself there is seeing yourself doing what it takes to get
there, as we are talking about long-term lifestyle change.
I revere people who have gone through significant physical transformation. To lose 100 pounds of fat or gain 20
pounds of muscle is just incredible. More than the change
in physical appearance, these people proved their mental fortitude, which is why so many of them continue on
from their personal transformations to help others achieve
the same.

I recently saw an app that ages you to see what you'll
likely look like in your seventies. I wish they had the same
for people looking to lose weight, gain muscle, or just be
full of energy. They could take the picture and tack it on
their bathroom mirror or refrigerator and practice literally
seeing themselves differently.

I had actor Josh Peck on my podcast in 2022. Josh became a famous kid actor in the Nickelodeon series *Drake & Josh*. In the beginning, he was morbidly obese, but he lost more than 100 pounds over the course of the show's run. In our conversation he shared that even though his physical reality changed, his mind still thought of himself as the slovenly, food-addicted kid he had been, and he loathed himself. Thus, the transformation didn't bring him the joy he hoped for; he didn't find joy in the achievement until he found compassion for his previous self. I'd encourage you to find compassion for yourself now if you're at a place where you are not proud of how you look and feel. You didn't know what you didn't know. You dealt with life as you understood it at the time. Now you have new information, new motive, and a drive to change things for your benefit. You are driven.

TAKE ACTION

Take a look in the mirror. Can you see yourself slimmer? Firmer? More muscular? Free of aches and pains? Feeling and looking vibrant and full of energy?

YOUR BODY ZONE

Motivation speaker and author Jim Rohn is renowned for his quote, "You are the average of the five people you spend the most time with." This may be most apparent when it comes to health and wellness. People habitually align with people who think like them, eat like them, and play like them. As I covered in the "Roadblocks to Avoid" section, striving to improve your health and wellness among family and friends who are not doing likewise can be very difficult. People often feel threatened when "one of their own" makes a positive move, as it can shine a light on their own shortcomings. Two things generally happen: Sometimes people can't handle the threat, and your positive change causes a breach in the relationship. More often, however, you will inspire them and help them feel like they have permission to make positive change in their own lives. Your attitude has much to do with it. I find most success comes from neither elevating or minimizing yourself and your new drive and direction. You are simply trying some new things. I've also found that people are much more eager to accept you stating you want to feel better than look better; it's hard for them to dismiss you when you say you're addressing some health issues and want to minimize aches and pains and have more energy. For some reason this is far less threatening.

For you, however, I greatly encourage you to find other people on the same journey. This again is why Weight Watchers (now WW) has such great, long-term success. It goes beyond a mere plan and brings people together. This is the same reason health clubs do so much business with group activities like Spin, Zumba, and yoga classes. The group encouragement and accountability is possibly more beneficial than the activity itself.

Want to run? Get with a running club. Cycle? Find a cycling club. Lose weight? Find a group in your area. I'm a fan of face-to-face, but you can of course subsidize with online groups.

Another staunch tool you can employ is a personal trainer, dietitian, or health coach. For some, this is invaluable and near vital. I've had multiple people on my podcasts, people who have achieved great successes, who admit they simply don't like physical activity. But they understand the benefits and employed physical trainers to help them. I had one guest who paid a trainer to show up at her home three days a week, even if the knock on the door woke her up and she had to answer in her pajamas. In changing diet and exercise, it can sometimes be challenging enough to make the change without having to manage all the details, so getting help so you can simply respond is often powerful.

CHAPTER SUMMARY

▶ **Case for How Your Body Looks and Feels:** How you perceive your physical self has much to do with your personal confidence and peace, as well as opportunity cost out in the world. How you feel physically influences every aspect of your well-being, which a recent podcast guest expressed as "Being yourself, well."

▶ **What Is Inherent:** Your genetics gave you some set points to how you look and feel. Strengths and weaknesses. Being aware of them will help you adjust accordingly so you can be at your fullest function and capacity.

▶ **What You've Been Exposed To:** Where your genetics influenced how you look and feel, your upbringing and environment greatly influenced how you *think* about how you look and feel. Give great consideration to how physical image and well-being was perceived, and then discern how you want to perceive it for yourself.

▶ **Roadblocks to Avoid:** Moving from a mindset of deprivation to delaying will serve you far better. Then, cultural pressures and expectations will often provide the most friction for your desires for increased health and wellness. Evaluate the state of your current environment and adjust to overcome any negative pressure.

▶ **What You Authentically Want:** We all want to feel good, but what things are you willing to accept about your body, and what performance are you striving for? How we look is generally only understood by how we attract other people, but the real power is in owning how we look and feel for ourselves.

▶ **What Motivates You:** How we look can fall victim to "shoulds" and the expectations of others, possibly more than in any other area of our lives. Get to the root of what motivates your pursuit of how you look and feel and your overall wellness. Know your motive and make sure you are in agreement with it.

▶ **See Yourself There:** Seeing yourself as looking and feeling better takes tremendous faith, as you are striving to see something different than what is in the mirror and feel something different than what currently exists within you. But what you can see and envision, you can become.

▶ **Your Body Zone:** If you want to change how you look and feel, you'll find no more benefit than communing with those who look and feel as you desire, and those who are on a similar journey.

CHAPTER 6

What Drives
Your Mind

You Are How You Think and Feel

A s much as we are enamored by the idea of human exposure to chemicals or radiation giving us superhuman powers, we are likewise intrigued by the untapped power of the human mind. One favorite depiction of mine is the 1996 fantasy drama *Phenomenon*. In this movie, George Malley, played by John Travolta, is an average man who works as a mechanic and chair maker. One night after his birthday celebration he sees a bright light in the sky that grows in his vision until he is knocked down by it. In the following days and weeks, he begins exhibiting unparalleled levels of intelligence, even resulting in telekinesis. Ultimately, it's discovered that he has a brain tumor whose unique placement and growth has triggered and released his mind's true potential.

In 2011, *Limitless* was released, starring Bradley Cooper. In this movie it's a nootropic, a smart drug that gives the character remarkable intelligence with perfect recall and the ability to analyze details with complete accuracy and at incredible speed. He goes from being a struggling author to acquiring great wealth and running for the US Senate in one year's time.

Both movies lend credit to the idea of our mind's untapped potential. While we know we're not limitless in our potential, we suspect we have a capacity much greater than what we make use of. The good news is we can massively expand this capacity without a brain tumor or super drug. The primary catalyst is simply what we believe about ourselves. This does not in fact make us limitless, however. Try as I may to believe I can flap my wings and fly, I will fail. But most of humanity is living at a belief level of sitting on the floor when we are actually capable of sprinting and jumping.

I'll ask you to reference the story of Victor Serebriakoff once again, from Chapter 2. It's profound to realize that Victor's life change did not come from suddenly acquiring any additional skill or ability. He had lived his entire life with an IQ much higher than anyone else he'd likely ever been in contact with, but he only saw and believed what he was told. When he received information that changed his belief, he simply agreed with his new "reality" and began living it out. We, in turn, must fully and readily accept that we are capable of performing at a higher capacity, as our capacity has few quantifiable limits. It is fluid and is primarily minimized or maximized by our perception and subsequent faith in ourselves. All Victor received was new proof that there was more in him than he had previously been told, and the result was that he instantly harnessed abilities that had lived inside him all along. When he saw himself differently, he started acting differently. He started expecting more from himself and began immediately benefiting from his enhanced perspective and resulting actions.

When someone offers, "Hey, you did your best" as a con-solation, or self-soothes with the claim of "Well, I did my best," it has always ruffled my feathers. I think my annoy-ance comes from my athletic pursuits, where I realize how much goes into top performance and I know I could always have done a bit more: better prep, better mid-race decisions, and even better effort. I don't feel the need to sugarcoat it by claiming, "I did my best"—I actually get more motivation by just admitting there was more I could have done, some-thing I can correct next time if I am motivated to do so. You may have made a valiant effort with great intent, but to say you did your best diminishes your chances at improve-ment and minimizes personal responsibility.

Right now, you are not doing your best or perform-ing at your best in regard to your potential and capacity. I believe this to be absolute fact, and accepting this statement provides you with more opportunity than any chemical, radiation, or super drug in the movies, because you can begin harnessing it immediately and there are zero nega-tive side effects. But there is a caveat generally missed by the self-help industry. Changing your belief about your potential and capacity will increase it a little bit. Most of the growth, however, will happen when you take action from this belief. Belief is simply the starting point. Believing you can run a marathon doesn't place you at the finish line, it just motivates you to step out your door and start training.

Most of us believe in our abilities, but only as it relates to what has already been proven to us. But was it a reflection of our best? The full possibility of our capacity? Or was it based upon our output due to the level of belief we had at the time? This begs the question, what more are we capable of if we free ourselves from the limitations of our belief?

Let's continue to use Victor's story as a muse. Imagine receiving a knock at your door, and lo and behold it's God.

Or Gandalf. Or your fairy godmother. The FBI. Whatever does it for you, but they reveal they been monitoring you for years and found evidence you are one of the most brilliant, gifted, insightful, and intuitive humans they've studied. They measure your mental and/or physical capacity to be 10 times greater than your current output. They are giving you one year to try to harness your actual ability and will then provide placement in a high-level position needing your leadership to help save the country and all human-kind. Wealth and fame and Nobel Prizes are assuredly in your future.

How would you feel about yourself from that point forward after you close your door? How would you conduct yourself? Your perspective just changed from however you see yourself now, to considering yourself to be a very highly valuable asset. Your chin is up, shoulders are back, and confidence is brimming. Your treatment and expectation of yourself would likely quadruple, and from that, everyone else would start treating you differently. Here is the kicker. I guarantee when the year is up you would find that you have already made more positive progress in your life that year than in the rest of your years combined. I should just hire somebody to come around and lie to everyone with such a story so they'd start believing in themselves and greatly increase their confidence, behavior, and results. Which would then make the lie truth!

With Victor, as I continue to take some liberties with how his story played out, we can assume the teacher pro-nounced him remedial due to his performance. We don't know Victor's full story and what might have played into his poor school performance, but I'm confident he wasn't "doing his best." Many highly intelligent people struggle with the rote structure of school. Maybe he was bullied.

Maybe he had a hard home life. Maybe he just didn't care. There could be any number of reasons, but we can assume the teacher showed him proof of his lack of ability from his schoolwork and test grades. It was not a true representation of his overall ability but simply based on the understanding and experience he'd had so far. Even if someone had later told him he was capable of more and tried to encourage him, he would likely have believed the proof he'd seen from himself. It's just reality, right? A reality he'd seen and he didn't know any better than to agree with. Seventeen years passed until the fateful test that showed him different proof. Victor believed he was lacking due to the "proof" he'd experienced, then when the so-called proof changed he believed he was a genius. His behavior changed for the better, thus his actions changed for the better, and of course his results changed for the better.

What proof about your ability and capacity are you believing? If you can right now acknowledge you have accepted a level of capacity for yourself that is far less than what is possible, you have taken step one. Step two is what we often miss. Now, you must train your capacity. Changing your belief about your ability and capacity won't change your performance overnight, and if you don't truly step in to do the work, it won't change anything much at all. In the world of personal development, we generally fail to present a true depiction of how it plays out. Victor had an IQ of 161, but in his ignorance he lived as someone with an IQ of 80. He passed the time with menial work and didn't challenge or work out his brain. Then the fateful day came and the truth was revealed of his superior IQ. While his vision and belief increased a hundredfold, his ability and opportunity did not change overnight. Now he had to put in the work to bring it to fruition.

Some of the greatest racehorses of all time such as Man o' War, Seattle Slew, and Secretariat were found to have hearts larger than those of their fellow thoroughbreds, and this anomaly was a factor in their success. But imagine they had been born on a farm and used for plowing, every day slogging it out in the mud and dust and never given the chance to run in the open pasture. Then Farmer Brown finds out his horse has an abnormally larger heart and enters him into the Kentucky Derby the next day. That horse with a heart of larger capacity than the others, able to take in and be fueled by much more oxygen, would absolutely get clobbered. That heart isn't used to the demands of racing. To get it into race shape and up to its capacity will take a long time of hard work and training.

Likewise, Victor's newfound revelation of his brilliance was in fact a revelation of the possibility of his brilliance, but then he had to train it. By my calculations, Victor was 15 when he was pronounced a dunce. So he spent the next 17 years doing various menial jobs. At 32 he was tested and found to be a genius. He may have been in the army at this time, and he left the army in 1947 at age 37 to go work in the timber industry. He did not join the Mensa society until 1949 at age 39, seven years after his revealing test. He had to work that brain out to bring it to its higher potential.

Merely realizing you have more potential does not make that potential possible until you start training toward it. Working it out. Potential is not a light switch, but a marathon. Motivational seminars and initiatives often deserve the criticism they receive, as they erroneously proclaim that belief alone is the difference. Belief only matters if we adjust course and do the work to earn the new possibilities.

Are you ready to believe in more for yourself and start training your potential and expanding your capacity? There is no greater opportunity to create drive than by harnessing and leveraging your mental state.

HOW YOUR GENETICS THINK AND FEEL

Kerry Ressler, a neurobiologist and psychiatrist at Atlanta's Emory University, conducted a study in epigenetic inheritance in mice. He wafted the smell of acetophenone around the mice while giving them small electric shocks. Acetophenone is said to smell like almonds and cherries, which would generally be rather nice; however, when it came alongside a shock, the mice just knew pain was coming. Imagine one of these mice taking a vacation in the countryside, out on a nice stroll with the family, as they come upon a cherry orchard, and all of a sudden this mouse freaks out and runs for safety while everyone else is basking in the great aroma. What is more astounding is that this fear of the smell was passed down to the mice pups. The pups had never been exposed to acetophenone in their lives, but when it was presented, they were shown to be extra sensitive and automatically moved away from the smell. But what's truly mind-blowing is that the sensitivity showed up in the third generation of mice, and even in mice conceived through in vitro fertilization with sperm from the original male mice.

Looking back at your biological grandparents and great-grandparents, what fears could they have passed down to you, particularly fears that pose no real threat to you today? Think about phobias we are so prone to accept, such as fear of heights or spiders or closed-in spaces. What might have happened to your great-grandparents that instilled this fear into your very DNA? This quote from Terry Real, who was on my show to discuss relationships, is profound: "Family pathology rolls from generation to generation like a fire in the woods, taking down everything in its path, until one person in one generation has the courage to turn and face the flames. That person brings peace to his ancestors and spares the children that follow."

Of course, this goes far beyond emotional transference and would relate positively to confidence and peace as well as cognitive propensity. And there is no objective reality. You could have come from a long line of miners who had great success and prosperity from their mining expeditions, and from it you feel great comfort and peace in closed-in spaces. Conversely, your family of miners may have known poverty, horror, and death from tragedy in the mine, and today you find yourself massively claustrophobic, just like the third-generation mice who are afraid of the smell of cherries. Think of this as your "emotional genetics."

We can also look at cognitive predispositions. Think about the cognitive environments of five generations of ranchers. People who lived in wide-open pastures with great big skies, taking care of cattle herds that spread over thousands of acres. The howling wind, thunder, and hoof-beats gave breadth to big sights and sounds. The day was spent looking far out over the land, traveling to and fro, cognizant of the weather and land and temperament of beasts. The day ended with physical exhaustion and most of the brainpower going toward big-picture thinking. Now compare this to a family of clockmakers in a big, compact city who worked down in a basement shop. Everything was tight and precise, from the surrounding walls to the deli-cate watch parts. The work was detailed, concentrated, and relatively quiet. Few days were any different than another. It was a life of methodical consistency. In both cases we have significant wiring of the brain for thought processes and cognitive pathways. Add into this the positive or negative emotional influences, and you will likely find powerful ingredients for some of your own positive and negative mental predispositions.

The healthy and more whole mental aspects of your life are simply to be grateful for and leveraged. You'll do well to cater to these qualities and engage with them as much as possible in your life. In the areas of unhealth however, this is time to take them captive and discern a plan of action, which also includes how important and relevant they are to your life. For example, I've always been a good bit squeamish about snakes, and living at 9,200 feet above sea level I enjoy a near complete lack of them. So I'm good with having a fear of snakes, as it's not getting in the way of living my life. But if you find yourself with social anxiety or unable to ride in an elevator, you may want to look at some help with reprogramming.

The most powerful category of cognitive bias and emotional genetics, however, is one of faith and belief—in others, and in yourself. These far supersede any genetic phobia or IQ level. If you came from a heritage of faith, positivity, and abundance, you have great privilege working in your favor. Realize how much you have to be grateful for, and leverage this reality to the fullest. You have great reason to expand your life and the lives of others.

However, if you come from a biological family history of much fear, negativity, and scarcity mindedness, then know you are in for some work. Again and again, this is a set point to deal with, not a limitation to accept. You can build a large, solid, and sustainable home in a tree, in the sand, over the water, or on the side of a cliff. But you'll need more planning, engineering, and investment in these cases than if you were to plop a house down on flat, solid ground. And this is the point.

TAKE ACTION

What are the likely fears and confidences from your biological heritage that may have no relevance to your actual reality today? What thoughts and cognitive pathways were likely planted into your genetics that may be helping or hurting you today? And most of all, where would you rate the faith/fear, positivity/negativity, and abundance/scarcity states of your ancestors?

HOW YOUR ENVIRONMENT
THINKS AND FEELS

In his book *Spark*, psychiatrist John J. Ratey cites the "snake and stick" syndrome, where especially in times of stress we have a natural inclination to identify something benign as a danger, such as mistaking a stick for a snake. In spending much of my life traveling at high speed on remote trails, this concept is very relevant. Especially with my aforementioned aversion to snakes. Thankfully, there are few on my high mountain trails, and regardless I was very privileged to have an upbringing that expected the best in most events. Nowhere in your life is this programming more tangible than in your childhood programming from your parents or primary caregivers.

You likely grew up in a home where the best was expected of other people, or the worst. We can very much boil it down to a negative or positive bias. One of fear or faith. What I want you to understand here is that both can be problematic depending on how you personally responded.

The greatest propensity is to simply take on and embrace what you experienced. If you were exposed to positivity, optimism, and faith, you will most likely follow this, to your benefit. On the other hand, if you experienced negativity, pessimism, and fear, again, following along is most likely, to your detriment. However, there is a hidden danger to rebelling against either one for the wrong reasons. I've experienced people fall and fail on both sides of the coin.

If you had overly trusting parents who were badly taken advantage of, it might have motivated you to become overly untrusting. Conversely, if you had overly untrusting parents and saw them miss out on the glories of life and relationship, you could polarize and become overly trusting.

It's no secret how much influence our parents, caregivers, and authority figures have in our lives. I've even found some people who were far more influenced by extended family members or teachers than whoever was primarily in their homes. And of the seven areas of fulfillment covered in this book, in no area are we more influenced than mentally. While we may find early on that we disagree with some aspects of those who are leading our lives, we are most prone to be influenced for better and worse by their mental perspectives. What we most often find is people giving an elevated status to those who led their upbringing and a great need to remove them from any pedestal, even one of villain and oppressor.

If you can't take the primary authorities in your life and see them as regular, imperfect people who were victims of their own influences, it's very hard to disentangle yourself enough to consider they may have been wrong, even completely wrong, in some of their primary perceptions of life. They had to be to some degree, as they are mere humans.

Admit some of the authority figures in your life were absolutely wrong—and forgive them.

This is time to take stock of all your relationships and
the mental health and state of those closest to you. To reference Jim Rohn again, "You are the average of the five people
you spend the most time with." Though it could be one person or 10, the point is to think of those people you are most
exposed to and consider their perspectives on life.

So, how can you surround yourself with people who will
help uplift and support your mental well-being going forward? By auditing your environment so you can be around
others who are uplifting and supportive.

Audit Your Environment

This section is labeled environment for a reason, and
nowhere is your overall environment more relevant and
influencing than your mental state. If you take an audit
of your environment, how is it helping or hurting your
healthy, faith-filled, and joyful mental state? Think through
things such as your:

- Home
- Family or roommates
- Neighborhood
- City and state you live in
- Place of work
- Social groups

I won't be so insensitive as to say if any of those aren't
a light to you, abandon them. I understand the trappings
of life and work and relationships. These are big, complex
areas with seldom easy answers. This is time, however, to
audit how they are helping or hurting your drive for what
you believe to be best for your life, and the lives of those

you truly care about. You have primary control over the growth of your positive mental state, but it will only come as a result of just that. You controlling it. This is your primary area of need for proactive, intentional decisions and action. And you are up for it.

TAKE ACTION

Were your parents or primary caregivers and influential authorities primarily fear- or faith-based? Did they lend themselves toward a life perspective of scarcity or prosperity? Were you taught things would generally work out, or to expect the worst?

ROADBLOCKS TO AVOID

Historically we have looked at our state of mind as pure happenstance. As if it's handed to us like the color of our eyes or just rains down like the weather. That it's not in our control. This falsehood has been a foundational argument since the dawn of time, and I'm just another in a long line of purveyors. In 57 CE the apostle Paul wrote, "Do not be conformed to this world, but be transformed by the renewing of your mind." It's typically followed with "daily." As in, you must renew your mind daily. Think of it as rebooting your phone or computer every day to get rid of all the junk and stuck programs clogging things up. In layman's terms, you must take steps to control your mind, or it will be controlled by your environment and your unfettered subconscious mind.

Thankfully, in the past five to seven years we've become more familiar with the concept of neuroplasticity. Let me borrow from the initial Wikipedia definition, which I believe gives justice to the term: "Neuroplasticity is the ability of neural networks in the brain to change through growth and reorganization. It is when the brain is rewired to function in some way that differs from how it previously functioned." In other words, your brain, and therefore your mindset and state of mind, is malleable. Think of your bicep. If you don't work it out much, it's not very big and not capable of a lot. If you put it in a cast, it will atrophy before long. But if you lift weights consistently to break down the muscle, and you engage in adequate recovery, it will grow back bigger. After a few months, you can have a sizable bicep that looks good and is capable of lifting heavy weights.

Your mind is no different. You work it out. You train it. You reprogram it. You happen to it. The alternative is that your mindset and state of mind is like a beach ball out at sea being tossed around in whatever direction the wind, waves, and occasional shark may bat it.

This is the primary roadblock people get hung up on regarding their mental health, wellness, and capacity. We don't truly accept our ability to grow our minds to be what they can be. I say this as a fellow journeyman. I haven't arrived at mental utopia overall. I have some areas of strength, some of relative weakness. I've been a lifetime athlete, and as of this writing, at the age of 51, I recently competed in a mountain bike race. For 15.5 miles and 1:16 I rode near my limit. The entire race was 10,000 feet above sea level, and we climbed over 1,300 feet on a particularly rugged path. If we look at the mental strength and fortitude for the performance, I am a mental rock star. A primary reason? I feel in control. It's my happy place. I have mastery and experience flow. Whereas just a week before the race, I was dealing with some family drama, two cars in the shop, and the internet being out in our remote home, and my anxiety was sky-high. I didn't feel in control, so my mental state was wavering. Likewise, you likely have areas of your life where you are doing well in managing your mindset and mental state. Then other areas where you're not so successful. Give yourself some grace, and get to work. The hope and opportunity is that you can craft your mindset and mental state, just as you are crafting your drive.

TAKE ACTION

Have you viewed your mindset and mental state as simply static? You got what you got? Do you see it like the weather, changeable on any given day? Can you accept that you have agency over your mindset and mental state, and start taking steps to claim it?

HOW YOU WANT TO THINK AND FEEL

We live in a culture that equates being busy with being important, even though for most of history, the trappings of success were time and leisure. Similarly, we find ourselves in a time when it seems in vogue to have mental instability. Think of how often, in your home, work, school, and social groups, you hear people attest to "freaking out" or having a near panic attack, almost as if it's something to be proud of. We expect to hear about the harried mom and the near-burnout dad and the anxious kids. When was the last time you heard somebody state, "Man, I feel really mentally stable and well. I'm so grateful!"

Every morning we wake up and decide what clothes to put on. What if you decided what mental "clothing" you wanted to wear on a given day? Can you imagine looking over your mental wardrobe options and deciding, "You know, today . . . I think I'll go with massive guilt. Maybe a bit of anxiety and some disgust. Yeah, that sounds good." As opposed to saying, "Today, I'd like to embrace confidence and peace, no matter what the circumstances are. I think a healthy side of faith in things working out and believing I'm OK is in order too. This is what I'll clothe and lead with today."

I don't say these things lightly and surely don't mean to trivialize life's traumas and stressors. But when was the last time you took your mental state captive and took decisive measures to be the person you want to be?

I am often interested in my children's mental imagery, and we'll often talk about what character they'd want to be from movies they've viewed or books they've read. It's an interesting exercise to watch them think, answer, and then explain. I've never had one choose to be an outright villain or a mentally unstable character. They generally choose a character of redeeming qualities and emotional strength. Why would we choose any different? The point is, we *can* choose. Do you want to be confident, at peace, composed, and above all the drama? Don't take "above" as superior, just as healthy and whole and able to thoughtfully respond to life instead of frantically and blindly react. If you say yes to this, then you know what direction to put your efforts, and in this realm of mindset and mental state, making an intentional effort at all is your first win, while the world around you bobs around aimlessly on the sea of emotional instability.

TAKE ACTION

What do you want for your mental state? Who and how do you want to be? What character in the story do you want to play?

WHAT MOTIVATES HOW YOU THINK AND FEEL

An all-time favorite movie of mine, and one I think is wildly underrated, is *Warrior*, starring Tom Hardy and Nick Nolte. It's a character study of two brothers and their alcoholic father, with the general backdrop centered around martial arts. In the movie, a celebrated trainer has his athletes come out to the "cage" to the music of Mozart, which is a stark contrast to the normal heavy metal or hardcore rap music you'd expect for a fight. His premise is that he does not want his athletes fighting from anger and raw emotion, but from a place of centeredness and control. The motive? Win the match.

In considering the mental state you desire, you will best serve your efforts by having a muse or goal. You can state, "I want to feel and behave this way, so that _____" and fill in the blank.

Years ago, while I was involved in a business advocating self-employment, I found myself among some out-of-balance events in my life and behaving in a fairly manic manner. My friend Randy asked me if the example I wanted to showcase to my kids was one of the entrepreneur leading a frantic and harried life. The question stopped me in my tracks, a callout that caused me to evaluate how I was living and behaving. It didn't solve everything immediately or even by today, but it gave me a focus, a goal: to live so that I'm a good, inspiring example to my kids.

As you consider the character you want to emulate, go beyond the image and ask why. This will get to the heart of your values and purpose, as it will likely draw you to consider the people you care about and how you want to show up for them. Though I also give you free rein to let your ego have a say, as it's a powerful tool. Thinking of the character you respect and would most want to emulate, can you think of how their values, mindset, and mental state influence those around them, to their benefit? I find myself drawn to Gandalf from *Lord of the Rings*, and Forrest Gump, by how living their values influenced those around them.

I've given you content here to draw you to the positive motive for how you want to think and feel. While I'm not calling you to dwell on and be dragged down by it, it's good to get the cards on the table by considering what is motivating your current and consistent mindset and mental state. Many of you, and to stereotype men in particular, will not be clear. I encourage you to be vulnerable here and give yourself compassion. You've likely accomplished a lot, doing the best you've known how. Me too. And we can grow from here.

TAKE ACTION

You want to have what mental state, so that _____?
What example do you want to set for others? Whom do you want to serve with your healthy mindset? Who is an image of a mental state you want to emulate, and why?

SEE YOURSELF THERE

If seeing yourself physically different is hard, seeing your-self mentally different is 10 times harder. But doable. Terry Real, whom I cited earlier, is an acclaimed family therapist whose fans include celebrities such as Gwyneth Paltrow, Bradley Cooper, and Esther Perel. In his book *Us: Getting Past You and Me to Build a More Loving Relationship*, he compares our "Adaptive Child" to our "Wise Adult." He explains that when we feel unsafe and threatened, we tend to act out as from our immature selves and the childhood adaptations we learned to survive. But when we are present and aware and can summon our faith and maturity, we can thoughtfully respond to life as the wise adult we have within us.

Terry shares a relevant visual from his own life:

> When my wife, Belinda, comes at me upset, I take my Adaptive Child, the little eight-year-old Terry, and in my mind's eye, I put him behind me, physically, where he can hold on to my shirt. I make a deal with my younger self. I say to him, "You can stay back there, and I'll protect you. Like Superman taking the blast with his spread-out cape, I'll take the brunt of Belinda's upset." That way her hurt and anger would need to get through me, my strong back, to get to my Adaptive Child. "So my part of the bargain is that I will protect you. Now, here's your part of the bargain. You let me deal with Belinda. Don't try to do it, okay? You'll make a mess out of it. I can deal with her better than you can."[1]

I find this concept not only very relevant, but possibly your only option to actually see yourself differently. Much attention is given to the concept of the higher and lower self, but if you look back at the past, whether it was 10 minutes ago or a few days ago, you will find times and events when you can recognize you were instinctually reacting as your Adaptive Child or thoughtfully responding as the Wise Adult. Work to separate them in your mind.

For example, take a look at a childhood photograph of yourself and see if you can recognize how that kid learned to adapt. Be compassionate and forgiving to that child, but recognize you don't have to succumb to what she or he learned all the time. As Terry showcases, you want to protect that child and grow beyond them as you start to see yourself, full-time, as the wise adult you can be. You can be. But just be aware and present.

TAKE ACTION

How did you learn to adapt as a child? How do you react when you are triggered and feeling insecure and unsafe? How do you react when you feel confident and secure? Can you see and separate out your Adaptive Child and your Wise Adult?

YOUR MIND ZONE

The number one asset you can have in striving to achieve a mindset and state of mind you desire is to find someone else who is there and can relate to you. Mind that last part, "and can relate to you." There is no greater power to your psyche than to find someone who "gets you." It's akin to nirvana to feel understood. But where do you find such a person? As mentioned earlier, there is great value in books and stories and characters you relate to.

However, the ability to truly resonate with anyone is massively helped by getting personal guidance to understand yourself, such as in counseling, therapy, or coaching. In fact, the best athletes have top level coaches on their team and go further to hire specialists on their own dime. The best businesspeople I know have business coaches. The healthiest people I know have health coaches. The people I know with the most solid mindsets and jedi-level states of minds work with mental coaches, counselors, or therapists.

Counseling is no longer for crisis. It's for wellness. And today we not only have many counselors and therapists to draw from, but a wealth of online resources, including some that are available remotely and nearly 24/7.

There are also great groups of people you can pursue who are mindset focused. Whether it's yoga or guided meditation, spiritual groups or athletics, find and surround yourself with people who are striving to be the best versions of themselves. I grew up in the entrepreneurial world and found the greatest value not from the exposure to business information, but instead from rubbing shoulders with people who expected more from themselves. Their drive, passion, and attitudes became contagious—and I couldn't help but be hooked.

Most people pursue communities for the information and end up staying for the relationships. So go find people who will lift you and encourage you and even hold you accountable to believing in more from yourself. This is coming from a thoroughbred introvert, and in regard to that, you will seldom find me at big gatherings and "networking" events, but I find what fits me. You can and must, as well.

TAKE ACTION

Have you or can you work with a counselor or therapist to best understand your current mindset and mental state as a starting point? Have you found someone who "gets you"? What groups might lend themselves to the desired mindset and state of mind you desire?

CHAPTER SUMMARY

► **Case for Your Mind and How You Think and Feel:** As humans we tend to accept what is showcased to us about ourselves, and this becomes our reality, when in truth there is no objective reality, but only our perception. We are not limitless, we can't be or do anything, but we are all functioning at a far lesser capacity than we are capable of. We must believe this and take appropriate action.

► **What Is Inherent:** Positive mental health we can be grateful for and work to leverage. But our negative mental perspectives likely trace back to our grandparents and great-grandparents and beyond and can very well have no relevance to our lives other than that our ancestors had reason to be fearful of something, like the mice with the smell of cherries, and it was simply passed on to us. It's time to check your limiting beliefs for whether they have any true justification and place in your life.

► **What You've Been Exposed To:** Your primary mental programming and state was formed in your upbringing, and it's incredibly hard to disassociate from the primary influences and authorities in your life. But you must. You must step back and consider the humanity and imperfections of everyone who has influenced you, including today, and consider yourself specifically and set apart from the relationships in your life in both the past and present. And likewise consider your overall environment and how it is positively or negatively influencing your drive.

▶ **Roadblocks to Avoid:** Your mindset and state of mind is not static. Neither is it happenstance. It's a result of your intention and preparation. You can grow, train, and change it just like any other aspect of your body.

▶ **What You Authentically Want:** You have agency over your mindset and mental state, but it will only come from you being present and taking captive what you want with as much clarity as possible.

▶ **What Motivates You:** Look to a character, an avatar, who emulates the mindset and mental state you respect, and seek to understand why you desire this, both for yourself and for others.

▶ **See Yourself There:** To see yourself with a different mindset and in a different, elevated mental state, you need to be able to see and separate your Adaptive Child from your Wise Adult.

▶ **Your Mind Zone:** You will be best served to get professional counseling and therapy to begin this journey. There are also great affinity groups once you know what you need. Find them and invest in them.

CHAPTER 7

What Drives
Your Work

You Are What You Do

If you were to ask someone from the Middle Ages all the way up to the mid-1700s, "So, what do you do?," you'd likely get a look of bewilderment, and quite possibly one of two answers. Either "What do you mean by asking what I do? I . . . live. Just like everyone else!" Or if you press for specifics, you'd get a long list; "I fetch water, plow, plant, hunt, gather, sew, wash . . ." and so on. Most people lived a very similar lifestyle of farming and making handcrafted goods necessary for life's very existence. While you might have someone with a particular skill like blacksmithing or making pottery, everyone was engaged in the same daily activities, which primarily revolved around the acquisition of food and shelter. Earning money to purchase items was a low priority, as you harvested and made most of what you needed on your own. Your vocation was making and procuring the necessities for your life. Then things changed.

The Industrial Revolution took the focus from making many things, to making *money* to buy all those specific things. And all those things began being made by specialists who crafted them in order to provide them to others and make money in return. It was a massive economic and vocational shift. It took families who used to work together away from their home and into specialized work roles. One year Dad is basically a farmer like every other guy, the next he has a specific role on an assembly line in Henry Ford's new car factory. Mom is of course at home, as only she can nurse the new baby. Soon Dad announces to his family and everyone else after a promotion, "I'm a manager!" or "I'm a drivetrain specialist!" and boom, that's the cultural dawning of attaching your status to the question, "So, what do you do?"

We could debate the health and even morality of this cultural evolution, but it would be beside the point of this book. Here my focus will remain on what *is*, and from it, what you want it to be. Work and vocation is here to stay. When someone asks me, "What do you do?," I've sometimes tried to buck it and respond with something intellectual and witty such as, "I create opportunity out of ideas!" Or more tactically, "I'm a father and a husband, and I mountain bike and have meaningful conversations." But it mainly just creates confusion, and admittedly, it's my cumbersome attempt at skirting the issue. It's hard to get around the notion that what we do is our primary social capital, the primary way people measure our credibility. We don't want to judge a book by its cover, yet we do, and in today's economy we really must. It's the system that has been built, and it won't go away any more than paved roads will. We all want to lobby for equality regardless of social status—but not many of us would hire a Realtor or lawyer who shows up driving a jalopy and wearing grungy cutoff shorts.

What we do will dictate how much money we make and how many opportunities we have. Period. And since we can't live outside this construct, it will have ramifications for our self-image and lifestyle design. The true value, of course, is not what we do but how we *feel* about what we do. We will spend a vast majority of our daily lives engaged with our chosen vocation, so if our duties and roles fall within our gifts, talents, and abilities we will likely find great purpose and fulfillment in our life overall. Conversely, if we grind out 8 or 12 hours per day doing something we do not enjoy, we will likely suffer to untold degrees, and it will be near impossible to live a driven life when for so much of our day, our hearts are parked. To try to negate the power and influence of what you do for work will be one of your greatest mistakes in life. Let me say it again: it's not what others think of what you do that's important, it's what you think of what you do that really matters.

I was given a silver spoon in this department in being raised by Dan and Joanne Miller. I never knew my dad to work at something he didn't enjoy and get fulfillment from, and in 2002 he wrote the bestselling book *48 Days to the Work You Love*, and he has been leading the charge for the "work you love" movement for decades. Both my parents did what was needed to put food on the table and clothes on my back, and there were times when this was a struggle. As a kid I didn't care, as the greatest value was having parents who were inspired and faithful about their daily endeavors. Their example contributed to my comfort with trying new things, being OK with failure, and believing things will work out OK. Thanks Mom and Dad.

What you do in your vocation will ultimately be one of the greatest contributions of your life, or one of the primary erosions of your soul. I don't agree with the idea of work needing to be play. As I sit and type these words, there is little I'd rather be doing otherwise. It's glorious. But it's hard work, not play. I'll go out and play on my mountain bike on a high mountain trail later. This is work. Wonderful, life-giving work.

TAKE ACTION

How do you feel about the work you do? Do you see value in it? Are you engaged in activities that feel fitting and fulfilling to you? Are you proud of your work and your role?

WHAT YOUR GENETICS DO

To point to two extremes that can serve as examples of how we might view our vocation, I'll again make reference to Ebenezer Scrooge, the old miser who pinched and counted every penny and accumulated vast wealth. Yet he spent as little as possible and lived the life of a pauper, returning to a cold, dreary, and dusty home every night to sit by a feeble fire and drink tepid soup all alone. Contrast this with the infamous parable of the Mexican fisherman who catches fish for the day, and when asked what he does with the rest of his time, says, "I sleep late, fish a little, play with my children, take siestas with my wife, Maria, stroll into the village each evening where I sip wine, and play guitar with my amigos. I have a full and busy life." He's encouraged by a visiting businessman to expand his business and create great wealth so at the end of his days he can then relax, sleep late, fish a little, play with his children, take siestas with his wife, stroll into the village each evening and sip wine, and play guitar with his friends. It's a legendary and profound parable. The fisherman is living the life he adores, but in our cultural construct he is encouraged to abandon it for years, decades even, so he can hopefully afford to come back to it. The construct is based on the assumption that he should get to a place where he doesn't have time for fun, as he's busy 24/7 working to stay afloat, and he must prepare for his old age when he will linger for years and need provision he can no longer produce. How did we get to this place?

Behind you are the generations of your grandparents and great-grandparents, and what is etched in your DNA is aspects of what they did, day in and day out, and how they felt about it. Did they sit at a desk in comfort and security, or was every day an adventure through the unknown, with discomfort and risk? Was the day fairly consistent or always changing? Was their lifelong vocation the same, did it alter some, or were there dramatic shifts? Roughly 50 years of daily toil will change your brain chemistry in regard to how you feel about it. Fifty years of harvesting crops, or on Wall Street, or in the military has a massive effect depending on the duties performed, the environment of the tasks, and your attitude about it all.

In all cases, did the daily duties and roles fit their natural gifts and talents? Or was their time spent doing things they had very little natural propensity for? Was the environment one of peace and joy, or drudgery? Were they more like Ebenezer Scrooge or the fisherman?

How did all your "grands" *feel* about what they did? Could they work at a high-pressure Wall Street firm with tyrant partners or bosses and be OK with it? It's unlikely, but for the sake of making the point, we'll allow it as possible. By the same token, could they have worked like the Mexican fisherman and possibly be wildly unfulfilled?

The combination of what they did and how they felt about it over a lifetime influenced their very DNA and was passed on to the next generation. This legacy does not necessarily dictate your ability to absolutely love your work, but it will likely influence your set point. As we discussed, that set point is a factor that can be a benefit to support you, or a bit of a handicap you'll need to take clear action to change. If you find yourself generally joyful and hopeful about your work, you may assume you have a history of people behind you who enjoyed their work, or the negative impact was fairly inconsequential. However, if you find yourself constantly frustrated, unsatisfied, and ill at ease, you may need to realize you need to take some positive action to reframe the purpose and opportunity of having joy and honor in your work. Finding work that accommodates your natural skills, abilities, and talents; viewing what you do as an expression of yourself; and making revenue to support you is a powerful thing. It's necessary if you want to live a fully driven life. Again, it's not what you do that matters so much but how you *feel* about what you do and why you do it.

TAKE ACTION

How have your genetics driven your perspective on work? In considering what you know of the three biological generations behind you, would you deem your genetic set point for work is helping or hurting you? How? If you had the fortune of a relationship with your grandparents, how did they speak of their lifetime vocations? Was it joyful and valuable, or nothing but a drudgery?

WHAT YOUR ENVIRONMENT DOES

The General Social Survey conducted a 40-year study to show our predilections for following in the work footsteps of those who raised us. For example, if your father was a doctor, you are 23 times more likely to follow in his footsteps, and 17 times more likely if he was a lawyer. This makes complete sense, and the tendency for many is to either follow in the footsteps of what we understand or rebel against it, both of which can easily lead us astray. In one of my favorite movies, *Forrest Gump*, Lieutenant Dan is depicted as coming from generations of men who fought on the front lines and died in various wars, and I can't help question whether each man in Lieutenant Dan's family was really designed to be a soldier. Maybe not, and that's why they all died. Even if they all felt a responsibility to serve their country, differing personality styles and inherent skills would likely have one on the front lines, one in communications, one back at the base driving logistics, another helping keep the tanks running, and so forth. This belies our propensity to follow in footsteps our feet don't fit within.

The influence of the work roles held by the authority figures in our lives is profound, and uncited in the aforementioned study is how many people end up pursuing vocations due to influences outside their nuclear family, for example, from extended family members, teachers, and even the parents of close friends. What's worth understanding is not only how what we are exposed to shapes our destiny, but also how great is the influence of what we are *not* exposed to, meaning our hesitancy or even complete ignorance to pursue vocations we have never experienced, a mindset that can be incredibly limiting. I see this with my own kids, whose mom was a professional performer and dad a professional athlete, who then worked within entrepreneurial realms with a variety of jobs and businesses that happened to strike their fancy. My kids have little to no exposure to professions like doctoring or lawyering, the corporate and executive world, or academia. Furthermore, they have little exposure to the lifestyles of those vocations. To then pursue something completely outside of their experience would be taking a big leap. My children's dispositions are heavily weighted toward their parents' example and worldview of work. This is a benefit to some of my kids and a handicap to others, depending on their natural disposition.

The workaday lifestyle our parents modeled for us will also likely become an expectation that can lead to disappointment, as today these influences extend beyond our personal experience and more from what we see in the media. Many kids hear very little about the workday from their parents but may never miss an episode of *The Office*. I was 18 when the *Dilbert* cartoon strip made its first appearance, which showcased an exaggerated and ludicrous, yet scathing view of the worst of corporate America. While both *The Office* and *Dilbert* may provide comic relief, they don't help instill a positive view of work as a contribution to the world, but rather a necessary evil and something to be tolerated in the quest to pay our bills and find some belonging.

I appreciate the autonomy of self-employment, as well as the risk of either great opportunity or spectacular failure. I like having multiple projects going on at the same time. It fits my personality, and from this, even though I can get a bit frantic at times, my kids know I get great fulfillment from my work. This is great for them, though again, it only shows a narrow view of work style.

The importance here is to consider the general attitude toward work you grew up with. Did your parents and their friends communicate that work was simply a grind? A necessary evil in order to make a buck and pay the bills? Was it looked at with more honor but still just something valiantly done to provide for the family and not something to necessarily be excited about? Or was it shown as an exciting arena of self-expression, personal progress, and social benefit? Did the authority figures in your life dread their work? Or tolerate it? Or find great joy and purpose in it? You likely had teachers who treated their jobs as a gift and offering to the world, and others as if their time in a classroom was a jail sentence, and they took out their despair and anger on the students. These perspectives no doubt influenced you, and still do today. Just like genetic predispositions, they'll serve you well when they're recognized as the benefit or detriment they were, so you may gratefully accept the positive or mitigate the negative.

I do want to be sensitive to the people who toiled away to provide opportunities for their children and endured a lifetime of showing up and doing what it takes. In our world today, however, there are near infinite options for work, and it's been well proven that the happiest, most contributing, and highest earning individuals spend their days working at something they enjoy and/or truly matters to them.

In 2010, Thomas C. Corley published his book *Rich Habits*, which was the result of five years of monitoring and analyzing the daily activities and habits of people both wealthy and living in poverty. His research revealed that 96 percent of the poor did not like what they did for a living, 86 percent of the rich liked what they did for a living, and 7 percent of the rich loved what they did for a living. Further Thomas cites, "The group who loved their jobs accumulated more than twice the wealth of the group that liked their jobs, and it took them about a third of the time to get there."[1]

And the proof for this doesn't stop there. In my young adult years I was very influenced by Thomas J. Stanley and William D. Danko's book *The Millionaire Next Door*, which revealed that most millionaires were not the doctors and lawyers, not the celebrities and pro athletes, but instead the everyday business owners working at something they enjoyed and were good at. These people find purpose behind the paycheck. If you need to work at something less than fulfilling for a time in order to survive, that's totally understandable. Kudos to you. I've done it as well—for a short time. During these periods you will serve yourself, those you care for, and the world far more if you take a second job called "Find a more fitting and fulfilling job." It won't likely find you, so you must go find it.

TAKE ACTION

How has your environment driven your perspective on your work? In considering your upbringing and the primary caretakers and influential people in your life, would you deem your environmental set point for work is helping or hurting your overall vocational drive?

ROADBLOCKS TO AVOID

No surprise here, the expectations and exposure of our parents, providers, and community is the primary detour taking us away from what might be the most fitting vocational direction. Some are blatant with outright pressure to follow the career direction of a parent, or to be involved in the family business, or even—conversely—the familiar story and expectation to *not* do something bigger and better. Either way, it's a significant pressure.

I experienced this with one of my kids who sheepishly said, "Look, Daddy, I know I could make more money doing my own business, but right now I am struggling to be self-directed and motivated and just want a job where there is some structure to follow." I felt so bad, realizing the pressure and expectation I'd put on him to do as I have. While I meant well, I was not being sensitive to what he was feeling at the time. The oft-cited Bible verse calls us to train up a child in the way they are bent. Zero in on how *they* are bent, not how *we* are bent or want to bend them. The pressure and expectation to attend college and choose a good career sends a significant amount of people down a blind alley, away from what would be fitting and fulfilling to them.

Parents, educators, and the traditional education system are also heavily prone to looking at what a kid is good at and encouraging, if not pushing them down this path. The "what they're good at" mentality has influenced hordes of people to pursue something they had a knack for, down vocational paths they didn't at all enjoy. Please hear this: being good at something does not mean we necessarily enjoy it and will find fulfillment in it. As a youth I was big, fast, and fearless, and had really good eye-hand coordination, thus excelling in ball sports like baseball and football. So I was greatly applauded for and encouraged to pursue an athletic career in these team sports. The problem was I'm not a great team player and often struggled with the culture of coaches and teammates and the antics of the locker room. I finally quit high school football to devote myself to my earlier love of bike racing and found my fit in a more individual sport where, honestly, I may not have even been quite as naturally gifted. But I was happier with it and therefore devoted more to it, and I found great success.

From a parenting perspective, my youngest son is so naturally fast at running and has a mentality to push himself, he became nearly unbeatable in cross-country and track races at a young age. We live 20 miles from the Olympic Training Center, and I'm thinking, *This is my athlete. This kid is a gold medal. This is a gift that can't be squandered!* But as time went on, he shared more and more his dread of racing and how much he abhorred the pressure. I strove valiantly to take the pressure off and have him find joy in running, but for him, being in races meant he had to go all out and win, and his heart's desire was simply not to race. Today he enjoys soccer and the camaraderie with friends and has no desire to pursue athletics long term. None of my kids do. As a lifetime athlete, have I failed at inspiring them, or rather have I given them freedom to be who they are, not who I am? But as a parent, I understand the pressure we often feel to bend our kids to certain pursuits, especially when we see talent.

Let me bring the story home for you. If you are good at relating to people and giving great speeches in your school classes, someone may suggest you would be great at sales. You also like music, so you get a job at a local electronics store and work the floor to help sell electronics. And let's say you hate it. Maybe it's the corporate structure. Maybe it happens to just be the current management and staff. Or while you do in fact like music, you have no interest at all in electronics. Thus, you decide you in fact are not good at nor do you enjoy sales, and you cross this one off. This would be akin to me taking my dissatisfaction in ball sports and giving up all athletic pursuits altogether. This would have been a faulty decision, as I adore the pursuit of athletic achievement. In this case you may be wildly happy and successful selling a product or service you really care about, alongside people you appreciate and enjoy, which will likely happen when you are joined in a common interest. Maybe the fit would be you selling tickets to music events. Or selling yourself as an artist. We are so prone to throwing the baby out with the bathwater and missing the opportunity to flourish in so many different water sources.

When considering what you want to do vocationally, while giving great value to your inherent talents, skills, and abilities, give equal value to what you actually enjoy doing.

The other primary roadblock is pursuing vocational pathways for the wrong reasons. We are all aware of the pressure to get a degree and/or pursue a career in a field based upon money, and thus the sea of people working at jobs and even running businesses who do not at all enjoy their work. We can put status right there along with money, as untold numbers go after professional and corporate careers for the status of the title alone. Or even the aspiring artist who simply desires to be seen as an artist even though they absolutely love dealing with numbers and would be a rockstar CPA or financial advisor. We so often find well-meaning people trying to fit the round peg of themselves into the square hole of a career, which either thwarts their success altogether, or amid so-called success they become bitter and eventually burn out. The key, of course is knowing your why, which we'll get to shortly.

TAKE ACTION

What roadblocks do you need to avoid for your work drive? In considering the common roadblocks above, where do you feel you may be at risk?

WHAT YOU WANT TO DO

Let's minimize the enormity of this concept right off the bat by asking, "What do you want to do *right now*?" We know most people will have many different jobs over their lifetime, from the odd jobs in our youth to the initial years after college or entering the workforce. But more and more we are seeing people having multiple careers. My friend Hermine spent 30 years working in corporate America, but left in her prime to get a degree in counseling and start a successful counseling practice. We've reached a time in our society where there is more grace and expectation for investing in a job, career, or business *for a time* and then going after something entirely different.

The greatest way to decide what you want to do career-wise is to truly know yourself. When you do, you'll be able to find the right work that fulfills you—and that could be within a wide variety of vocational opportunities. For example, I've now started 19 business initiatives, and while they might all seem different on the outside, all but a few saw me in roles using my primary talents and desires. Whether it be a cycling team, an entrepreneurial community, or my podcast, each of those ventures has helped me to inspire people to live and be driven by their values in order to lead an inspired and fulfilling life. So take the pressure off yourself in finding one holy grail of work and instead get to know yourself and what drives you—and let that be your guide. With this in mind, you won't need to devote yourself to one opportunity for your entire existence.

If you are just entering the workforce, you may be finding it difficult to decide what you want to pursue for your life, as you haven't experienced much life yet. Your first step is to do the work to understand yourself and your natural talents, abilities, and joys, and then start trying things. Get exposure to as many work roles and environments as possible. Ask your elders about their experiences. If you see an interesting job or business, go audit it and see what it's like in the day-to-day.

For those of you who are already entrenched in the workplace, I recently asked this question as a topic for a show: What was a primary influence(s) for the current career/job/business you are in right now? It was interesting yet fairly concerning to hear that many people aren't readily aware of what got them into what they are currently doing. I discovered that for many it was just an available opportunity with little relevance to it being a real fit for them. How many career directions have been chosen based on a financial expectation of a certain annual amount of income, then determining what careers will support this? If you personally think $70,000 per year is a decent salary, then you might not even consider becoming a lawyer, even though it may be a brilliant fit for you. Or I may feel the need to make a quarter of a million or more annually, and thus automatically disqualify a sea of wonderful vocations that may not have this earning potential. It reminds me of the community social media posts I see from people in need of money saying, "Looking for work, will do anything." This is one step above standing at an intersection with a cardboard sign, yet it's the equivalent of what many do as they look for work that fits their expectations of a respectable or required income.

We tend to view our work opportunities only through the prism of our current experience, understanding, and perceived knowledge and capability, which then affords us the possibility of a scant fraction of the relevant opportunities available to us. For many, this can feel overwhelming, but again, to the extent you can understand yourself and your core strengths and what fulfills you, you can discount a great many career directions, but also open up to many you would never even have considered before. Why work at what you merely fell into when you can fully fall into the work you will flourish in?

Be bold enough to step back and consider what you want from your work life. Do you want to settle for mediocre, or have the courage to reach for a career or business where you would serve the world and express yourself to the fullest? Step one is believing it's possible; step two is to start doing the work to explore and consider your options.

TAKE ACTION

What do you authentically want for yourself within your work? What activities do you enjoy? What roles actually fit you? Have you viewed your opportunities with a fairly narrow perspective? Be bold and don't discount anything.

WHAT MOTIVATES WHAT YOU WANT TO DO

We're looking for the reasons driving you and the emotions behind them, and as I've covered, many of us approach our work with the same barely veiled drudgery we had in completing the household chores our parents required of us. Working because *we have to*. Let me just say that nothing of any lasting value has ever come from this perspective.

But there is value in reviewing the jobs you've had up until now and considering how you felt about each of them, including any odd jobs of your youth. This exercise will give clues to what motivates you. Many of us were first inspired to work in order to earn money for a desired possession. For me it was a bike, and I restored an old motorcycle and sold it to buy my desired BMX bike. While I did not much enjoy the work, I was motivated to spend my Saturday mornings working on the motorcycle while my friends were watching cartoons because I was envisioning myself on the bike. The tragedy and errancy would be to find me 10 years later restoring motorcycles because it made a buck, instead of racing bikes, which is thankfully where I landed.

Maybe you had a job at a camp where you saw the fruits of your labor in little kids' happy faces and your duties took on more meaning than whatever income you made. I experienced this at my aunt and uncle's camp, and at the end of the summer, my fellow camp counselors and I donated all our earnings back to the camp, as we saw the profound impact it was having on inner-city kids.

Go through each job and ponder why you were doing it. What were the payoffs? Do this all the way up to now. Why did you take the job you're in? What were the hopes? What inspires you to get up each morning and go to work? We're trying to find motive beyond money and putting food on the table. While again, I'm not criticizing this—it's a valiant effort for a worthy cause. But I am absolutely warning you that you'll never find fulfillment if these are your only reasons for working. Steady boredom and dissatisfaction will bleed into every other area of your life. You simply spend too much time and effort at work for it not to be negatively or positively programming your brain and overall inspiration and drive for life.

The question is, how do you feel about your work? Then ask yourself, how do you *want* to feel about your work? What would drive you to feel a positive emotion for waking every morning? If you have any thought that feeling good about work is just a luxury, you must eradicate it. It is a lie. Bottom line: ultimate vocational fulfillment is only possible when you feel it's more than just earning a paycheck, when you are contributing to or helping support something greater than yourself.

TAKE ACTION

What is motivating what you want for your work? Money? Status? Expectations of others? What work activities give you fulfillment? Where do you get lost in your work? What have been your most enjoyable work activities thus far? What negative agreements about work have you made, such as it being simply for money and you should be grateful you even have this job, even if it's harming your mental health and potential?

SEE YOURSELF THERE

To take an extreme example, let's say you are currently an executive making a solid six figures and you want to pursue being an artist or musician, or just start a small business. Now I know many artists and musicians who make far more income than some C-suite executives, and of course hordes of entrepreneurs are making millions and billions. The point here is dealing with the perception, however. Can you see yourself not waking to an alarm clock and donning business attire and commuting to a high-rise office, but instead waking to your own schedule, living in jeans (or whatever your flavor), and being completely responsible for every decision regarding your livelihood? How will your friends, family, and colleagues view you? Most importantly, how will *you* view you? I've seen this scenario play out and cause strife and failure due to nothing other than the person never being able to envision themselves in this new paradigm. That romantic notion seemed to go against their self-image.

Let's flip this scenario: If you grew up lower or middle class, saw your parents and primary social groups working fairly low-level jobs, and your perspective of economy is blue-collar, and you find yourself interested in being a doctor or lawyer or bank executive, there will likely be a struggle to truly envision yourself in such a new lifestyle.

This is big medicine, friends. We have so, so many people with a legit desire to pursue an ideal in their heart and mind, but it falls on unfertile soil if you really can't see yourself in this new reality. If you find this might be true for you, the question to ask yourself is, Why not? Why not you? With all due respect, there is someone out there in that role with less going for them. I don't offer this to shame you but to empower you. Most of the obstacles we see are self-imposed and merely perception, not truth. So, try to make a case for why you can't do whatever you have a fancy to do. Convince me, and in the process you'll likely realize most of your excuses don't hold water. Yes, you may have some things going against you that can make the journey more difficult for you. I don't discount this. But you know it's possible.

If you can't see yourself there, do you feel it just must happen anyway? Take the movie script of a character in a low-income family, in an environment where no one has ever made something of themselves. That character has no concept or exposure to anything beyond the neighborhood, yet in a poignant scene, their mother with her dying breath says, "Pamela, promise me . . . you'll make it out of here. You'll become something better. You'll show all the family they can be and do more. I see the spark in your eye and the ability in you, Pamela. Do it for me. For the family, for yourself!" This is just a plea. It's no proof of Pamela being able to do or expect more. But she looks around at the squalor, and contrary to everything she knows, she doubles down on her schoolwork and is the first to even apply for college. She's doing it out of a conviction, in spite of no true vision. She doesn't even have an example to draw from. It's completely unknown. But something has to change. And so, it does.

TAKE ACTION

Can you see yourself having the work you desire? Can you see yourself in a new or different role? Doing new and/or different activities more fitting to you? Or do you have enough conviction to take action regardless of your faith and sight?

YOUR WORK ZONE

As in Pamela's example, sometimes you just have to carry on without a real vision, but only a conviction to change. This is definitely difficult—there are certainly easier ways to get to success. The best way to reorient your perspective is to go rub shoulders with the people who embody the success you want to achieve. Going back to my example of the executive versus the artist: If you're the executive, when everyone heads to the swanky martini bar when they knock off work on Friday night, you go to the local artist dive instead. If you're the blue-collar gal, when everyone heads to the local watering hole, you get dressed up and hit the high-end club. (This is coming from a guy who can count on one hand how many bars I've been in, and the wild Friday nights of my youth were generally spent eating Ben & Jerry's, reading Stephen King, and going to bed early for a 100-mile training ride or race the next day! I went from this to a family and am ignorant on the night life of any demographic.)

To take an example from my own life: One time, in my quest to raise my own financial prospects, I attended a wine tasting by a financial management firm, which required that I buy a $300 case of wine. It turns out the clientele were mostly older and I should have found a more economically relatable group of younger, hungrier individuals, but those wine bottles at home still worked to keep elevating my perspective of how I wanted to see myself.

Find people who are involved in the vocational zone you are interested in and spend time with them. Ask a successful executive, artist, or business owner to coffee or lunch (you buy!) and state you want their advice and counsel. You'll be amazed at who says yes, as one, it's very hard to say no to a request for your advice, and two, most people are eager to impart what they've learned, though few are ever bold enough to ask them.

Often kids will attend college and earn a degree in a field without ever talking directly to someone who has succeeded in the field. Without ever taking the time to visit an office where this business is taking place. Can you imagine a boxer training for years by themselves and never being in the ring with a legit opponent, then stepping in one day for an actual fight? So go! Get in the ring with people doing the types of work you are interested in. Talk to them. Visit those businesses. Remember, you don't want to go against the flow of where you are currently. Get rid of this paradigm. You want to find a new, better-fitting flow to go with.

TAKE ACTION

Where is your work zone? Where might you find it? Make a list and don't discount anything.

CHAPTER SUMMARY

▶ **Case for Work:** Your work, the daily activity you engage in for a majority of your waking hours, matters immensely. It shapes who you are and how you view yourself. The daylong toil will shape you, for better or worse. Don't take it lightly as just something you do to make a buck.

▶ **What Is Inherent:** The generations that have worked before you have an influence on your current working life. To what degree, nobody knows. But it is worthy to consider the work and vocational attitude of your ancestors, and whether it's provided a boost or some friction to the feeling you have about work.

▶ **What You've Been Exposed To:** Think about your upbringing, and if it was positive and supportive to what you want for your work. If so, be grateful for it, and build upon it. If it was negative, then take action to reprogram your paradigm.

▶ **Roadblocks to Avoid:** Work is a primary category where we often fall in line with the expectations of those closest to us and the culture we were dropped into, not by choice. Realize it has limited your scope of possibilities, and make an effort to see beyond it. Work is also a place to find yourself striving from a hidden motive attached to your identity. Get aware.

▶ **What You Authentically Want:** What work do you want to do, free from the limitations you have accepted thus far? While you can theoretically strive to do anything, you can't do everything well. But within your gifts and abilities and joy, there is far more opportunity and possibility than you have ever imagined.

▶ **What Motivates You:** As you zero in on the work you truly want to do, be keenly aware of the emotion behind it, and be in agreement with it. While pain and fear can be strong motivators for work, make sure you understand and are at peace with your motives.

▶ **See Yourself There:** You'll serve yourself best to be able to envision yourself in the work position you desire. Not authentically seeing yourself there will likely thwart your efforts. If you find this a struggle, ask yourself why. An alternative is finding a reason strong enough to override your self-doubt.

▶ **Your Work Zone:** One of your strongest medications for gaining comfort and confidence with a new work role and environment is to go engage with it, in any way. Read about the vocation and lifestyle. Watch documentaries. Go visit this style of business in person. Ask someone involved to meet with you, ask their advice, and interview them for testimony.

CHAPTER 8

What Drives
Your Money

You Are What You Have and Don't Have

I n 1992 I met a guy who had been making a load of money in real estate by borrowing money and leveraging it. Until the banks called in his loans—then he went bankrupt. The emotional turmoil that resulted from that failure motivated him to write a book to try to help people find freedom with their finances. He also started a radio show on the topic. My wife and I were this guy's first employees, helping him sell and deliver books, run his business, and hold live events. We worked out of his home in the cheap seats of Nashville, and we often watched his kids while he and his wife worked on the business or went on an occasional date. He led a class on money for the premarital class we attended at our church. The guy's name? Dave Ramsey. The little blue, self-published book back then was called *Financial Peace* (I still have a couple of those original books somewhere), and the radio show was *The Money Game*. Today, of course, Dave is the most well-known name in America regarding money matters, and his podcast is one of the most listened to shows in America, with many millions of listeners for every episode.

While Dave has done a world of good for a mountain of people, 30 years later we find the grim statistic that one in four Americans say they are very anxious about their money, and over half admit that money controls their lives. If there is any aspect of life where we seem to be fairly driven, it's with our money, but more often than not, this drive is not so healthy or fulfilling.

It's not fair to simply focus on money in and of itself, as it's merely a representation of what we can and can't afford and the possessions we do and don't have. Therefore, to have a valid discussion on the matter we must take a hard look at the money you make, the things you purchase, and what you own.

At its core, when we are talking about money, we are really talking about safety, security, and opportunity. I've always abhorred reality TV shows, but my friend Todd talked me into watching a season of *Alone*. This is the one where participants are left solo out in the wild in an attempt to survive for 100 days. Very quickly they come to find what is of true value: things like warmth, not getting sick, and finding food. Specifically food with fat, which was of great interest to me. The items that helped them procure these things were their greatest assets—worth their weight in gold, truly. The arrow to kill a deer, the hook to snag a fish, the sleeping bag for warmth at night, and the flint to make a fire were truly priceless. These items were their relative money, and it was literally the difference between life or death (though in this case, they could tap out and be rescued by the TV crew!).

At our core, the things we feel we need to survive are absolutely vital to us. While you may be someone who has luckily never been truly concerned about starvation or finding a place to sleep, that type of pressure is life-altering. A 2018 article from the Aspen Institute explained that "the potential of suicide increases among financially distressed individuals as debt levels become harder to manage."[1] The threat of not being able to support yourself and your family, and the immense cultural pressure to be successful with money, is nothing to minimize. The latter may be greater than the former for you, which I address later in this chapter in "Roadblocks to Avoid." Again, it harkens back to our genetic hardwiring for survival. The cavemen feared their food and home being stolen; farmers feared drought and destruction; and today we fear creditors and the mortgage and social embarrassment.

To compound this fear, we surround it all with our work and "what we do," which is inextricably tied to our self-image and worth around what we can afford and what we own. We are a culture that gives credit to those with money, and disdain to those without. We can criticize this mindset, but as humans we can't help but make quick judgments that sway us toward or away from people, at least initially. Whether you are on Wall Street or in Beverly Hills, in the Bronx or in a hippy commune, you will find favor going toward the desirable level of abundance in a particular culture. We can attach ourselves to the car, watch, jewelry, trendy clothes, or even outspoken, pious frugality. I've not met a person yet who is unaffected by a financial persona.

One of my first podcast guests was Rabbi Daniel Lapin, a prolific author and speaker and an advocate of making and having money. His definition of money did more for my perspective around it than anything else I'd heard before, as he labeled money as a "certificate of appreciation." Meaning, if you go forth and provide value to people in your work, you should receive appreciation in the form of compensation. You learn this early on. After all, my friends never volunteered to mow any of our neighbors' yards for free. But they would gladly do it for the "certificate of appreciation" of 5 or 10 dollars.

This can sometimes create friction, though, as there are many people—all of us, at one point or another—who believe that they're providing relevant value but feel they're not getting equal appreciation in the form of the compensation they deserve. The bottom line is how we place value on the ability to hunt and gather, whether that "hunting and gathering" is the show of appreciation that affords a second home or luxury car, or the recognition of employee of the month at a modest job. The main question is: Can you go out in the world and come back with provisions for yourself and others? We can't escape the fact that a healthy portion of our personal well-being and our cultural status hinges on our purchasing power and possessions, which all boils down to money.

I find most people are polarized: they either really like money or really hate it. And generally, those who like money have more, while those who hate it have less. To get to the bottom of where your drive is as it specifically relates to money, we'll have to explore the emotions and motives you have around it.

For instance, I often find people who claim to hate money, but they love to purchase tickets for live concerts and pay for dinners and drinks. They also love owning a bike, a car, a smartphone, and a purebred dog. Claiming you hate money but adore what it buys is like hating water but loving to swim. What they *hate* is really the effort to get it, keep it, and manage it. I will not give one iota of financial advice here, as this is my Achilles' heel. I'm an artist who just wants to create things. The 19 business initiatives

I have started were, in essence, just art projects to me. I'm a poor businessman and a less-than-stellar steward of my own money. My point in this chapter is only to unearth how you view and feel about money, so your drive produces what you actually want. We're talking about the *why*.

WHAT YOUR GENETICS HAVE
AND DON'T HAVE

Downton Abbey is the most-watched series in PBS's 45-year history and provides a wonderful look at how money, possessions, status, and individual perspective are passed down, both literally and figuratively. The show depicts gentry and royalty who are grateful for and generous with what they have, and others who are spiteful toward those who have just a little less and hoard what they have. You see the same polarizations of perspective among the servants. And generally, these perspectives are passed down accordingly. The wealthy landowner whose ancestors were generous continues on in generosity, while the wealthy hoarder passes down these hoarding tendencies.

Look back to the generations in your family before you. Regardless of their position of great wealth or relative poverty, what was their attitude about what they did and didn't have? Have those perspective passed down to you—knowingly or unknowingly?

Investigating this may reveal unexpected clues to some of your own perspectives and propensities. So many of us are often perplexed and unsure of where our attitudes come from toward these aspects of our lives, and we don't see these as genetic set points.

Not everyone will be able to find stories or documentation from their family's past. (In fact, I haven't really been able to myself.) However, any knowledge you can gain of who came before you, any awareness of your own propensity, and any clarity you can gain to understand what you may have adopted as your own because of your family will help you get clear on what you truly want. And from that awareness you will be set up to adjust accordingly.

TAKE ACTION

What kind of work did your grandparents and great-grandparents do? What style of living did they afford? How much did they leave behind? These can give clues, but if they're still around so you can ask them directly about attitudes around money, you'll hit the jackpot.

WHAT YOUR ENVIRONMENT HAS AND DOESN'T HAVE

In the previous chapter on work, I cited the tendency for us to follow in our parents' footsteps vocationally. We also tend to follow along regarding money, possessions, and social status. And if you didn't follow their lead, chances are you simply reacted out of rebellion. Either way, you were undoubtedly influenced by the lifestyle and financial status of those who raised you.

From the 200-plus guests I've had on my podcasts, all of whom have achieved significant financial success, I've heard a sizable number of men explain that they felt, even as children, that they needed to make a lot of money to escape the poverty of their childhood. Likewise, many guests, in this case both men and women, had experiences of a parent who was hurt by a lack of money, and they vowed to make money in order to care for them. While both are good motivators to earn more than they grew up with, they are reactions to pain and may not be pure and healthy drivers leading to true fulfillment. Likewise, it's hard to find real peace if your primary motive is to prove others wrong or "show them what I'm made of."

Conversely, people born into wealth make up very little of affluent culture today. Whereas the pain of poverty can motivate action, wealth often breeds inaction from comfort, or again, a desperation to hang on to what one has due to lack of faith in one's ability to procure more.

Interestingly, in affluent cultures, I find more and more people with a fair level of ambivalence toward money. Their upbringing was middle to upper-middle class, and the lifestyle was neither frugal nor lavish. Money wasn't much discussed in their family, so these people come out with very little drive, other than to maintain a comfortable lifestyle.

The place to start is to take stock of how the topic of money and the rules and expectations around purchasing and acquiring possessions were treated during your childhood. Here I'll briefly touch on five categories for you to consider when it comes to your parents' or primary caregivers' impact on your views when it comes to money and possessions. There is overlap, but I'm looking to uncover the nuances you may have experienced.

Scarcity or Abundance

Stark statements such as, "You don't get something for nothing" and "There's no free lunch" set up a zero-sum mentality surrounding money. Scarcity mentality hinges on the notion of needing to hold on to what you have, and take what you can, because resources are limited and finite. Taken to its extreme, this mentality can lead to things like hoarding. On the other side is a perspective of "there's plenty to go around, and more will find its way to you when needs arise." It's a win-win mentality and one of generosity and a belief that the more anyone has the more everyone has. If I have two things and you have none, when I give you one of mine it's not a loss on my part, but a gain for us both.

Fear or Faith

This is fairly similar to the above, but there's a subtle difference. Even in a scarcity mentality I've found some folks who still have faith that things will work out and they'll do what it takes. Whereas with deep-rooted fear, there is the true concern of ending up in dire straits regardless of a reality of abundance. This is acute for me, as I have an abundance mentality but have always had some anxiety around it. I remember thinking I'd feel OK if I made six figures. Then I got there and realized it made no difference to my feelings, as they weren't based on an objective reality but some ingrained emotions.

Control or Generosity

In our historically patriarchal culture, many people have experienced control issues around finances, usually coming from a father who was the sole provider for the family. Money was used to manipulate and put everyone else in their place (think of statements like "you are eating my food!"). On the flip side, generous providers might treat the money as more of a communal benefit (perhaps signaling the sentiment "this is our bounty" while saying grace before a meal). These are wildly different perspectives on how to feel about money. Were you made to feel guilty for your desire and consumption, or were things provided with grace?

Bitterness or Joy

Some have ended up at a place where they have a visceral hatred of money, so they treat it like an enemy. Dave Ramsey has said that money is like a brick. You can build an orphanage with it or throw it through someone's window. The question is our attitude. Bitterness is a common emotion we have toward money, whereas some treat it with pure joy. When we work at something that gives us little to no fulfillment other than the money we make, bitterness grows in us and we adopt a victim mentality. It gives us a sour perspective toward money. Whereas when our work provides far more to us than mere money, we find ourselves feeling good about the money we receive as a wonderful by-product of our joyful contribution.

Social Status

Simply understanding the culture you experienced growing up, whether it was poverty, middle class, wealthy, or anywhere else on the spectrum. You may have experienced more than one status, going from "rags to riches," or from having it all to having nearly nothing. Subconsciously, you accepted the status you experienced, or you rebelled, perhaps disavowing poverty or wealth and the trappings of both.

Use the same categories we just discussed to consider how your family, friends, and social groups have generally viewed money, purchasing, and possessions. Whether or not you feel you already have a handle on these issues, I encourage you to audit your current environment and think about what's working for you. Are your influences from your family and peers affecting your finances for good or bad?

TAKE ACTION

After carefully seeking awareness of your past and present environment, how do you feel about your current money situation? Proud? Shameful? Fearful? Faithful? Do you feel secure in your ability to procure what you need for the life you want? How do you feel about the possessions you do and don't have?

ROADBLOCKS TO AVOID

The primary roadblock to your overall monetary drive is summed up in one name: Jones. As in, "keeping up with the Joneses." My wife and I used to babysit Dave Ramsey's daughter, Rachel. She's all grown up now, and I had her on my podcast. She talked about her book, *Love Your Life, Not Theirs*, where she showcased the alarming trends in economic pressure people felt solely from striving to attain the same status as their friends. She showcased the damage social media has done in giving us daily doses of what everyone else has and is doing. The highlight reels of life. And we now compare ourselves to everyone all the time. You put a kid of any personality type in a new neighborhood and school, and you'll quickly find them desiring to buy the same items as their peers. We all desperately want to belong.

Not long ago, some affluent outdoor enthusiast friends of mine were talking about a favored brand of sunglasses, and I found myself feeling I needed to get a pair. Then I reminded myself that I actually don't like wearing sunglasses and rarely ever do. How many times do we find ourselves buying or desiring things solely to fit in when, if left to ourselves, it's not a purchase we'd ever make?

It's tempting to criticize affluent social groups where there seems to be little individuality. Big house, late model car, designer clothes and jewelry, and exotic vacations. There are homeowners associations that control everything down to whether you can have a garage sale or not, and if you do there is a dress code. But even without HOAs we generally find the same trends from house to house. Similar makes and models of cars, same size TV screens, same grills, even the same sports and hobbies. In contrast, I enjoy the mountain towns around the Rockies where you find truly economically eclectic living: you can have a $10 million luxury "cabin" with another million dollars' worth of toys next to a 50-year-old double-wide trailer with a satellite dish in the front yard. It's rare, however, as we tend to emulate each other to a drastic degree.

Of course, we know birds of a feather flock together. But regarding money it can provide an undue pressure on finances that is truly harmful. I've got to hand it to Mr. Ramsey again for nailing it with this quote: "We buy things we don't need with money we don't have to impress people we don't like." The question involves looking at your money and possessions and questioning how true it is to your authentic drive and desires, and how much is influenced by social expectations. Unfortunately, many of us can look at our spending styles and material possessions and point to a good number of things we purchase just to fit in or impress others. I admit, I'm not immune to it either. Though I'm not an avid consumer of normal amenities—I drive old vehicles, wear clothes till they are truly worn out, and generally don't upgrade anything until it dies—I'm self-conscious about my old, decrepit grill on the back porch. I don't use it a ton, and truth is, it just does what it's supposed to do. The only reason I'd cough up hundreds of dollars for a nicer one is for appearance's sake. I was offered a friend's fancy grill and decided to decline, just out of principle that the other one still works and I'd hate to chuck it in a landfill. Same with my old trucks. We live in a national forest, and I'm often hauling lots of kids, lumber, trash, or bikes. Anything that doesn't hold a lot is wasted on me, and cars up here get beat up. So why replace my 1999 Suburban with the immensely cracked windshield? I'm tired of buying new windshields that just get dinged and cracked again in a month's time on our dirt and gravel roads. That said, I still fantasize about buying that Porsche Cayenne, even though it has little practicality for my life. But I'd sure look cool. Maybe when some more kids move out of the house . . .

Let me not, however, discount opportunity costs. I'm happy to drive my old trucks, but if I were to decide to pursue a career in real estate, I would need to upgrade for credibility's sake. If you want to be taken seriously in the corporate world, there is an attire that's generally expected. You can go in the other direction as well. I had a good friend who made a fortune in wholesale furniture sales. I remember seeing his Honda Accord under the entrance to his multimillion-dollar home, and I questioned him about it. He said he spends time on the road going to many small-town furniture stores, and to show up in a luxury car would be off-putting for his clients and hurt his credibility. So hat tip to looking the part for whatever you want to pursue.

TAKE ACTION

How much of your monetary expenditures have been made primarily in relation to what other people see? Are you in agreement with it, or do you realize it was simply in response to the pressure of expectations? How much influence does your environment and social group have on how you perceive and handle your money?

WHAT YOU WANT TO HAVE

The exercise of asking yourself, "If I were the last person remaining on Earth, what would I want regarding money, purchasing, and possessions, now that nobody else is around?" doesn't quite work here, as you wouldn't need or care for much of anything but survival. So let's adjust it to, What if you woke up in a new city and could completely remake yourself? You choose the socioeconomic status you desire and what you buy and purchase. You can also think of the type of work you would do, and the income it would provide. It's a faulty notion to assume everyone would just be a billionaire with a mansion, yachts, and an infinity pool, as there are many people who have no attraction to this kind of lifestyle, or the people who run in these circles.

I knew a wealthy man who strove for riches and achieved them, leaving him with many millions and no need to generate money again. He fired his lawn people and bought a riding mower so he could mow his own yard. This was shocking to me as at the time, I had zero money and an absolute loathing of lawn mowing. I would have taken that money and paid any amount for my lawn to be cared for.

We'll shortly address the very relevant issue of social status, but for now try to separate yourself from your current environment and expectations and be free to look at what you *authentically* want financially. This will be hard, as we very much perceive of ourselves in the socioeconomic environment we've known. If you are wealthy and hang with wealthy people, you feel pressured to have the fancy car even if in truth you are not motivated to have it. If you are young and eschew consumerism, you embrace an old car even though you are actually drawn toward a nicer, more reliable car.

First, look at the money you earn: how much would you like to make? You must stay within the realistic limits of the work you want to do. If your heart's desire is to be a schoolteacher, there is a viable income level you can expect, even if you desire more money. If your dream is to be a doctor but you don't like the trappings of wealth associated with the profession, you'll have to figure this out. But if you could choose a level of income commensurate with the vocation you choose, think about what this would look and feel like and allow yourself to be open to it being quite different from where you are now. If you make $40,000 per year but truly would choose to be at a quarter of a million, free yourself to be honest. And vice versa, if you'd rather lead a more simple and austere life, allow the thought.

Regarding purchases and purchasing power, be free again to stay true to yourself without the pressures of your current environment. If you woke up in that different life, but magically could quickly have friends and loved ones, consider what your purchasing habits would be, especially on the expendable side. Consider whether you'd consistently buy coffee from the local shop or make your own, or whether you'd eat out nearly every night. Would you regularly purchase new clothes and gadgets, or not? Are you the kind of person who would choose to spend money on entertainment and travel? Be free to be eccentric and inconsistent, as most people with a healthy financial drive are. I've learned to be at peace and not justify my own idiosyncrasies. I seldom buy new and nice clothes, but I like quality new shoes that support my athleticism. While I'm generally prone to camping and love getaways in remote areas where I just sleep in my van, I'll sometimes splurge on a luxury hotel with all the amenities. I laugh at my contradictions, and just accept them.

Possessions are a key component of our relationship to money, and people struggle to really discern what they would have without the pressure and expectations from others. Again, put yourself in that new environment and question the housing, automobile, clothes, gadgets, and recreational items you would authentically want. Though again, I invite you to veer from strict constraints. You can live in a million-dollar home but appreciate the character of second- (or fifth-) hand furniture. Or live in a rented apartment but drive a luxury car. Wear thrift store clothing but a $500 watch.

This exercise is incredibly powerful for finding true and healthy drive around money, as it is far more than a mere exchange mechanism for goods—it's a lifestyle.

TAKE ACTION

Can you conceive of what lifestyle you would choose to have if you could start fresh? How much does it differ from your reality now? What would the cost and risk be to start living more authentically regarding your money and social status? Your socioeconomic bent?

WHAT MOTIVATES WHAT YOU WANT TO HAVE

Here's an insider tip on finding the best up-and-coming athletes. Their gear is worth more than all their other worldly possessions put together. As a lifetime elite cyclist, I know the best competition at a regional race will come from the dude who pulls up in a $3,000 car and a $10,000 bike. And chances are, 95 percent of the bike was given to him by a sponsor. That's the guy who is hungry and fast. His purchases are primarily motivated by performance.

What motivates our financial decisions spans five categories: status, self-image, performance, utility, and art. Socioeconomic pressure, or status, generally prevails as our number one financial motivator as a culture, and as part of the human race we can't and shouldn't fully disassociate from social influence. In this exercise I want you to authentically consider the motive of your financial decisions as they fit into these five areas.

First, let's look at your job. How much of your choice of career was relevant to what you really wanted to do, and how much was because of what it paid? The money you make matters, of course. But how much of the equation was it? It's not a fully fair question, but if not for the money, would you be doing what you're doing? We're trying to gauge how much of your work is attributed to money alone instead of contribution and fulfillment. Did you take the job for social status? The position and title your self-image desired? Was it because of performance and the chance to challenge yourself? Maybe it was purely utilitarian, or a pragmatic decision: it was work you could do, it was decent pay, and the commute wasn't bad. Or was it for art? Did it primarily fill a creative desire? None of these are intrinsically good or bad; the exercise is simply to make you aware of what you've done and consider if it's truly what you want overall.

Second, when you think of how much money you want to make, get to the emotion or desire driving your intent. You can't just say you don't care because you do! It's also unhelpful to simply say you'd of course like more. To say "more," you must state why and get to the heart of the purpose. "I want to make more money so that _____." Fill in the blank. And look again to our five categories of status, self-image, performance, utility, and art. Even if you feel your primary desire is to make money for the support of others, this still falls within your self-image. You want to be the kind of person who helps and supports others. This may be great for them, but it's rooted in how you desire to see yourself.

For your purchasing habits, strive not to be judgmental toward yourself. There are times when it's a great status move to pick up the tab for everyone's meal. In regard to our vocations, there are often times to spend money on performance. "You've got to spend money to make money" in your business is so often very, very true. Many people tend to feel guilt for spending money on themselves, even when it goes toward filling them up so they have more to pour out to others. If that message rejuvenates you, it's money well spent to give those you care about a more relaxed version of you. If buying some new appliances would alleviate some frustration, do it for the sake of those around you who could use you in a more peaceful state.

As you consider possessions you already own, I find it most helpful again to look at it from the vantage point of "I am the kind of person who owns _____, so that _____." We have stark imagery and association in our minds toward possessions. Most consumer items in our world today are sold solely from an aspect of association. The car ad sometimes tells you absolutely nothing about the quality or value of the car and only gives you imagery of four-wheeling in the forest, frolicking at the beach, or zipping along the Pacific Coast Highway. It's hard to make a case for any product being the best, and we have near infinite options from different manufacturers and brands. Picture in your mind's eye the stereotype of someone who owns a luxury car, a grill, a canoe, a cat, or a guitar. You get a mental image immediately. So then consider yourself and why you have the items you have, why you don't have some items, and why you might want others. Ask yourself what need they fill between status, self-image, performance, utility, and art.

One more highly relevant issue surrounding the sensitive emotions that drive our relationship with money is to look at the spectrum between love and hate. I struggle to find satisfaction on either side. People who healthfully appreciate money have known that it can be a double-edged sword, whether they live a frugal or lavish lifestyle. If someone claims a full-out love of money, I often find that they're compensating for the shame they feel in their pursuit of it. For those who claim hatred of money, I generally find they're bitter at the struggle they've endured around it, but in their heart would just like to have more money and less fear. This is a time to come to grips with your emotions, motives, and ultimate drive behind the often volatile feelings we have about money.

TAKE ACTION

Looking at what you currently own, what emotion led to the purchase? What things do you not own that you think you should, and why? Thinking from a socioeconomic standpoint, where do you feel comfortable?

SEE YOURSELF THERE

Sam Walton, founder of Walmart, was once America's richest man, able to afford anything. Part of his legend was that he didn't change his lifestyle. As he amassed billions he continued to live in a modest house, drive an old pickup, and have breakfast every morning at a second-rate hotel. It's not his frugality I esteem but his peace with his personal image. He grew up a farmer and found no reason to abandon the lifestyle he loved. On the other hand, I know many stories of people who came from poverty and could see themselves living a life of abundance. They took appropriate actions and today have million-dollar homes and live lavishly and find themselves full of gratitude and peace for their realities.

Now that you've determined what you want as a financial reality for your life, we look at your ability to see yourself there. As I mentioned, we closely associate ourselves in reference to our socioeconomic status; this exercise can sometimes be best addressed by asking yourself where you *can't* see yourself.

The psychology of this tactic can be seen with lottery winners. Search for "How fast do lottery winners go broke?," and you'll see studies showcasing that 70 percent lose or spend all their money in five years or less, and they are more likely to declare bankruptcy within three to five years than the average person. Why? They could not see themselves as wealthy people and thus could not support the lifestyle. It's cognitive dissonance. The same thing generally happens with people who inherit a lot of wealth. This is why building wealth slowly works, as you can adjust your self-image along the way.

If you are currently making $40,000 a year and you see the next promotion to 10 times your income, beware. That is likely too big a jump to make. To go from $3,000 per month to $30,000 per month would leave most people in the same predicament as lottery winners. I don't say this to dissuade you from the goal of a drastic increase in the money you make, but to showcase the very real gravity of achieving a different level of financial status. Until we change our *mental* reality, we will struggle to change our *actual* reality. It goes the opposite way as well. Take someone who has achieved wealth, and even if they lose everything, you'll find them back on top again relatively quickly.

Again, the point here is to find where you are truly at peace and where your authentic drive is. I like the mental game of considering if you suddenly had $10 million in your bank account, what would you do? How would you live? What would really feel comfortable? Sam Walton lived it out, and his answer was, nothing would change. As my personal income has increased, I've done very little to change my lifestyle and have put my money into caring for my big family and growing my business. I don't dream of a splashy car because I can't see myself owning and driving one—it doesn't fit my mental image. I'd challenge you to take some of the things you think you want and tangibly envision yourself there. Is it truly comforting and peaceful, or would it in fact be stressful?

I will add that if you feel discomfort thinking about living in a new financial reality, it doesn't mean you can't and shouldn't find comfort there, and the best way to do so is in the following section.

TAKE ACTION

To change your financial reality, you must make peace with how it would actually look and feel. Can you see yourself living a different socioeconomic lifestyle? Does that purchase you think you want actually feel good when you imagine yourself living with and among it?

YOUR MONEY ZONE

From 1984 to 1995 there was an American television show called *Lifestyles of the Rich and Famous*, hosted by British reporter Robin Leach, whose signature wish for viewers was "champagne wishes and caviar dreams." It was quite a curiosity to see the often ridiculous amenities afforded with vast wealth, whether it was a garage full of pastel-colored Rolls-Royces, solid gold toilets, or a fully rotating master bedroom. While millions of viewers tuned in, the attention proved to be more akin to a freak show than anything inspirational. I've visited grand mansions and garages with scores of luxury cars, and my primary feeling has been "what a grand hassle." But this comes from my personal economy of what I'd rather spend my time and money on.

I'm fond of wine and have attended highbrow wine tastings and events. Nothing wrong with them, but I'm aware it's not really my crowd. My inspiration is a killer mountain bike race or trail run with adventurous friends who celebrate the day's effort with a great dinner and wine. No right or wrong, just me.

To find where you are inspired and attracted socioeconomically will require you to experience those environments. The truth is, we seldom experience different environments, and to do so requires some effort. Few people from lower to middle class backgrounds have attended brunch or a soiree at a high-end country club or high society gala, while few of the upper class have attended an authentic backyard fiesta or rodeo. We tend to be very timid with exposing ourselves to other social circles.

If you're a banker dreaming about the life of an artist or musician, go out and rub shoulders with them. It will likely be uncomfortable at first, but in order to discern whether you could find comfort in this culture, you've got to experience it firsthand. If you want to taste higher society, you will need an invitation, or you can pay for the opportunity. Personally, my tactic has always been to seek out one person who has connections to the culture I want to experience, and get a personal invite. I'd encourage you to risk asking, and I bet you'll find people eager to expose you to the groups they are involved with.

Outside of personal connections, there's no end to clubs, organizations, and events for any interest. Conventions, conferences, and trade shows offer many venues to experience various levels of financial and social groups. When I was a teenager, I experienced many automotive trade shows and the lifestyles and trappings of those in the culture. As I've shared, I'm not a car guy, but even back then I knew I wasn't attracted to the industry and the lifestyle that went along with it. It was wonderful exposure, however. A few years later, I went to bicycle conventions and trade shows, where I felt more at home, even though sports and athletics were not anything my parents had ever participated in.

Be open to rubbing shoulders with other social groups and cultures and finding an attraction that you haven't yet been exposed to. You may just surprise yourself.

TAKE ACTION

What social groups have you been exposed to, and how did you feel among them? What areas and cultures are you interested in, and how could you gain access to rubbing shoulders with them?

CHAPTER SUMMARY

▶ **Case for Money:** Money is mainly about purchasing power and possessions. It gets to the root of your safety and security, and your cultural status, no matter your demographic.

▶ **What Is Inherent:** Looking back on your family history, was there a certain mindset regarding money, possessions, and status? Was there a fear or a faith? Getting to the heart of what money meant to your family can be a real game changer for adjusting your attitude around finances and can give you insight into some deep-seated values you've held on to, but may no longer be serving you.

▶ **What You've Been Exposed To:** You can't escape the impact from the attitudes and behaviors toward money and finances displayed by your parents or primary caregivers.

No matter whether you accepted them or rebelled against them, they served as examples that have driven your life thus far.

▶ **Roadblocks to Avoid:** Socioeconomic pressure is the greatest impediment to authentic financial drive and is your greatest danger to finding your own fulfillment in this area of life.

▶ **What You Authentically Want:** You will be best served to disassociate yourself from your past and current environments and tune into your true emotional connection and attractions regarding the money you earn, how you spend it, and what you own.

▶ **What Motivates You:** Tune into the motive for your money. Are you driven by status, self-image, performance, utility, and art? Taking a deep dive into examining your motivations will help your primary values rise to the surface.

▶ **See Yourself There:** It's very difficult to change your financial reality if you can't adequately envision what it would look and feel like to realize it. If we don't work on deliberately shifting our perspective, we generally settle to the level we are already accustomed to.

▶ **Your Money Zone:** We see ourselves in regard to how we earn money, make purchases, and what we own. A powerful tool to help us adjust our thinking and to find where we are truly inspired and attracted is to experience other social groups and cultures.

CHAPTER 9

What Drives Your Achievements

You Are What You've Achieved

As mentioned in Chapter 4, Bronnie Ware was an Australian nurse who spent years caring for people in hospice. She cited that the most common regret for the dying was "I wish I'd had the courage to live a life true to myself, not the life others expected of me."[1]

In 2022, I had author Daniel Pink on my show to talk about his book *The Power of Regret*.[2] While Bronnie's research was with the dying who no longer had time to correct their regrets, Dan studied a broad spectrum of people from all walks of life, many of whom did still have time to make corrections. He found all regrets fell into four categories, one of which he titled "Boldness Regrets."[3] Dan explained this is when people realize they aren't going to be alive forever, and wonder, *When am I going to do something? If only I had taken the chance.* They are at a juncture in their lives when they can play it safe, or they can take the chance. When people don't take the chance, they often

regret it. He went on to share that even in follow-up interviews with people who took a chance that didn't work
out, they were generally OK with it. At least they did
something.

The topic of our "dreams" gets much attention in the
world of professional development, self-help, personal
growth, and motivation. Yet I find that when we talk about
dreams, we are really referring to achievements. And these
provide a great source of drive both in the past and the
present. We often define ourselves and take pride in what
we have achieved and find a primary daily inspiration in
what achievements we are working toward and looking forward to. Conversely, without much achievement behind us
and in not looking forward to any, our overall drive takes a
massive hit in every part of our lives.

Every day I receive queries from authors, publishers,
and agencies desiring to get people on my podcast. Each
inquiry leads with two things: the focus on the person's new
book and their bio. What's in the bio? Their achievements.
What's in an obituary? A list of achievements. What's in
your résumé? Your list of achievements.

I recently rewatched the 2013 movie *The Secret Life of
Walter Mitty*, starring Ben Stiller. In the movie he's trying to fill out a profile on a dating site. He gets help from
an employee to punch up his description, and what surfaces is . . . he hasn't done anything. Literally, not much of
anything.

Now, before you object to the notion of judging someone's value by what they've done instead of who they
are, let me point out that you judge yourself by what you
have and haven't done as well. Note again the research on
regrets. You want to be a good person, and you want to do
some things that truly matter to you. For many people, the

actual answers to What is the meaning of life? and What am I here for? are simply to have meaningful relationships and achieve some worthy pursuits. It's not a competition of achievements, but a gift to yourself.

I was at a big mountain bike race recently, and the premier event was a 50-mile event over rock-strewn mountain passes at high elevation. Four hundred and thirty people lined up. The winner finished in a raging time of three hours and 35 minutes. Thirteenth place finished over 30 minutes behind the winner, and the last finisher was over five hours later. A few people were racing for prize money; the rest were simply there to prove something to themselves and accomplish something they were proud of. This is what funds prolific biking and running events all around the world. For every one person competing for the podium, there are a thousand there with only one purpose: to achieve something that makes them proud.

To really put this into perspective, let's take a look at an example of someone who is trying to get in better shape. While walking a 5K may not be impressive among runners, for someone who is using the event as their first step to improve their health, even walking that distance is a huge accomplishment they can feel great pride in. Picture that same person signing up for a second 5K, and instead of walking, they ran the entire time—slowly, but they did it nonetheless. That would still be progress that results in a grin as they cross the finish line, and it is solely for them. They did something great—they made progress!

This accomplishment of going from not taking care of themselves to walking a whole 5k and then completing the same distance while running will leave that person feeling inspired by their personal achievement—and the whole world benefits from their inspiration. They think of themselves with more confidence and ability. They think, *I'm the kind of person who does 5Ks. I have the ability mentally and physically to train myself and traverse 3.1 miles under my own ability.* They become happier, and they inspire their parents, spouses, friends, coworkers, managers, and bosses.

As Sheryl Crow sang to us, "if it makes them happy (and doesn't hurt anyone), it can't be that bad." In fact, I'd kick it up a notch and say it's downright glorious.

While athletic pursuits are easy muses for achievement, they are just the tip of the iceberg. The 2007 movie *The Bucket List,* starring Morgan Freeman and Jack Nicholson, shows the lives of two older men who are facing the end of their lives and want to accomplish what matters most to them. Like many people's bucket lists, theirs consisted of experiences, not achievements. However, the majority of great experiences entail doing something out of the ordinary and out of one's comfort zone.

Other popular bucket list items I found on top searches among a variety of lists include running a marathon, going on an African safari, learning to play a musical instrument, and skydiving. All are activities that require an investment in money, time, and discomfort. And they can all be put in the bucket of things that would make someone feel accomplished and proud of themselves.

Yet often the achievements we are most proud of are not the grandiose, high-flying adventures, but the events of our life that hold significant meaning for us. It might be winning a sporting event as a kid, getting into a certain college, landing a job, getting married, having a kid, starting a business, or writing a book. Again, try to refrain from comparing or concerning yourself with what others may feel is worthy. This is for you and you alone. Looking back on the next year, are you OK if you haven't achieved anything new? How about in five years? Ten? If you knew you'd die in five years, what would you want to show for it? I know it's a morbid exercise, but it's necessary.

Then there is the reality of how our accomplishments give us credibility in the real world. Back to the story of the author bios that get sent to me daily. They *do* matter. If someone hasn't accomplished much and there's little testimony from people wanting to hear what they say, it's too labor intensive for my team and me to vet them, so we just pass and look at the next one. The business owner or HR manager's job is far easier if they see some accomplishments, whether it is success in a previous job, a degree from Harvard, or even that you made all-state on your football team. Anything stands out other than, "I finished high school and successfully fulfilled positions at these places of employment." The value to yourself and the world of some worthy accomplishments in your life pays a far greater return on investment than an initial investment in Tesla. Maybe. Either way, it's incredibly powerful.

WHAT YOUR GENETICS ACHIEVED

For most of humanity there was great honor, or shame, based on the accomplishments of a family line. More important than inheriting money or belongings was the legacy of what the people had done. Even as recently as the mid-1900s most people were well aware of the history of their grandparents and great-grandparents and knew of their achievements. They were documented in their obituary and told as tales at family gatherings. Of course, this was a double-edged sword. If you find out your great-grandmother was a saint who saved a small village, you may feel pride in your family. If, however, she was a convicted axe murderer, you'll question the value of this knowledge. If your great-grandfather was a bestselling author and then everyone in your family leading up to you was a bestselling author, does it give you a legitimate advantage toward being a bestselling author? Let's look at some possible factors.

Confidence is mental, and as we covered in Chapter 6, is primarily based on your decided faith in yourself. We tend to believe what we see. Put a kid in kindergarten, and you quickly get reports on what they are initially good and bad at. "Jenny is incredible in art and English but really struggles with math." The minute Jenny hears this, she has confidence in art and English, and she has doubt when tackling her math homework. Generally, this sets her course from day one, and she tends to give more effort toward art and English and shies away from math, therefore supporting the initial testimony. But let's say the truth was that she did well in art because the project was drawing a unicorn and she'd recently done it at home with her aunt. And in English they read *Little Red Riding Hood* and were asked to explain it, and her dad happened to read it to her the night before, so she was well-prepared. In the math segment she actually got so distracted watching a little boy sneak candy from his pocket that she didn't have time to finish. But by then the die had been cast, and for most of the year Jenny will do better in art and English than math because the initial report caused her to give more focus and confidence to the areas she received praise and affirmation in. Now hopefully over time her true gifts will emerge, but examples like this happen all the time.

So back to my original question. I would think having bestselling authors in your bloodline can give you confidence to write a book yourself. But is there a legitimate genetic advantage in the literal fluency of words and comprehension and creativity? Does your brain truly have a greater capacity for authoring? I'm not sure this has been or can be proven, but I'd venture to say it doesn't hurt. There is some evidence to the aspects of the brain that were used most, which again, I referenced in Chapter 6. If you come from a line of career fighter pilots, the areas of the brain responsible for eye-hand coordination, quick mental calculations, peripheral vision, and managing high anxiety are very likely to be honed well and passed down, just like the mice who passed down a fear of the smell of cherries. This part of the brain is the cerebrum. Whereas a career author would be working out the areas of the brain responsible for creativity, imagination, and memory, which is said to be more in the hippocampus.

The moral of the story? Having great accomplishments in your past shouldn't hurt. They likely give you an advantage and predisposition for a specific area of expertise, but I'd venture to say even the mental fortitude of achieving success in one area is going to benefit you in pursuing high achievement in any area.

Today it's reported that only half of the population of America is relatively fluent in the history of their families. While genetic testing can give information on race and health, it provides nothing regarding the history of an ancestor's life. Thus, we have less than half of Americans cognizant of any family legacy, good or bad. This leaves a void, as we all have an innate desire to know where we come from and attach to the positive attributes of our bloodline. It's what drives adopted adults to seek out their biological parents. Even if they have no desire for a relationship, many at least want insight into who the parents were.

TAKE ACTION

What achievements have been accomplished in your bloodline? What stories were told or what was written in your ancestor's obituaries that can give you clues to your own propensities? If you don't know or your family hasn't accomplished much, the reason you are here, reading this book, is because those accomplishments will start with you.

WHAT YOUR ENVIRONMENT HAS ACHIEVED

The statistics I shared in Chapter 7, specifically focusing on work, showcased the tendency to follow in a parent's vocational footsteps. Much of this is simply due to a parent's accomplishments giving their child a perspective of *permission and possibility*. If you come from a blue-collar culture and suddenly announce you want to be a doctor, it may not be received as well as you'd imagine because it's a goal that's completely out of context for your parents. So they can't comfortably advise you on how to pursue and engage with that goal. They'd likely be more comfortable encouraging their progeny to be a mechanic or mason or welder. But for the kid whose mother and grandfather were doctors, it's much easier for them to embrace the idea of following that path. The way has already been blazed for them. Likewise, take the kid from the academic family who says they want to become a car mechanic. They'll likely be met with bewilderment, as their family has no understanding of the vocational path and lifestyle.

My grandmother was an English major and published some poems. Her daughter, my mom, has authored multiple books, and my father, Dan Miller, is a multiple times best-selling author, speaker, coach, and podcaster. Most of my career has centered around efforts from my writing. I speak, coach, and podcast. Both of my siblings are in similar fields of influence. I already have children who are avid writers and express a desire to write and create and influence others. My wife is published in multiple research papers. We talk about writing, books, podcasting, and influence social impact often; it's part of the family landscape and my kids feel comfortable with the idea of these vocational pursuits. None of my kids, however, have considered astrophysics, and the fact that I know nothing about it, except for how to spell the word, is probably a good reason why!

Following the same line of thought, how many people have been empowered by the accomplishments of a sibling, close friend, or extended family member? Statistically, when someone scores a high achievement, we see those closest to them either find permission to also become a high achiever, or else they feel threatened and distance themselves, as they don't want to feel the pressure to achieve more. You, of course, are the former.

If no one in your upbringing or environment achieved something qualifying for cultural high achievement—they didn't win any big awards or weren't ever recognized for any specific accomplishment—you can still glean something from their positive qualities and outcomes. Maybe someone just had a really solid and successful career or raised some well-adjusted kids. Maybe they served in the community and elevated a lot of lives. Look to hobbies and interests and areas where they invested themselves. Don't discount the concept of things they tried and didn't succeed with. The fact that they stepped out and tried is an achievement in itself. The mother who tried starting five different businesses and never gained much success still showed courage to even give it a shot. We're looking here for examples of grit and fortitude, optimism, and perseverance. The father who lost a child and grieved, but recovered to continue on, is a massive achievement you can embrace and use for your own way forward.

TAKE ACTION

Are you aware of the achievements of your parents or caregivers? Even if they haven't had so-called high achievements, what are some of the fruits of their lives you can identify?

ROADBLOCKS TO AVOID

A decade ago, I was part of an organization of high achievers. I'm not going to name the organization . . . and I'm not going to identify the person I'm using for this story. Because what I'm about to share is honest, but admittedly feels a bit mean. Most everyone in that organization I considered fairly intellectual, self-aware, and competent. But there was this one individual . . . (again, I ask forgiveness) . . . who was fairly clueless, socially and personally unaware, and even relatively arrogant. This person ended up achieving more than nearly anyone else, and what occurred to me was they were too ignorant to know they couldn't do it, and thus they just did it, while the rest of us stood around and intellectually discounted our efforts. From that experience I came to the conclusion that the more intelligent and self-aware people are, the quicker they are to discount themselves. They are smart enough to know the challenges and possible problems, and from this insight, they often don't even try. It was an irritating realization because it was all so true. We'd often be more well served by ignorance

If your mama told you that you were special, like Forrest Gump's did, she was right. Not more special than anyone else, mind you, but special in certain areas. I have nine children. If I did a broad spectrum test on them, would I find they are all, or any of them, truly above the average of overall humanity? I'd love to think so for my parental ego, but I'm not so confident. However, I do believe every one of them would score above average in some specific talents, gifts, skills, and abilities. Thus, overall we don't come out better than anyone else as humans, but we can be better at a certain endeavor. In this I'm a stout believer—everyone has a greatness in them. No more greatness than anyone else, but a different greatness where they can stand apart and excel. So instead of being on the side of doing great things because you're greater, or not doing anything great because you aren't great, is doing a great thing in your special area of greatness. That is something we are all capable of, and I believe destined to do, if we'll accept it.

The primary obstacle to accepting greatness in yourself and ability for high achievement is being accountable to it. One of the most popular motivating quotes of our time actually pinpoints it, but I think people miss its gravity. Author and political activist Marianne Williamson famously said, "Our deepest fear is not that we are inadequate. Our deepest fear is that we are powerful beyond measure. It is our light, not our darkness, that most frightens us."[4] That resonates deeply with me. If we accept it and proclaim our capacity to achieve great things, we open ourselves up for failure or at least disappointment. We inherently think it's safer not to try. We tend to look at trying something new and assess the risk of doing it. We fail to flip the perspective and consider the risk of not doing it, effectively staying where we are. More often than not the negative consequences of doing nothing are greater than those of doing something. It's what all the research on regret shows: what we regret most is what we have not done.

"Shoot for the stars!" they say. The closest star, Proxima Centauri, is 5.88 trillion miles away. So far NASA has "only" made it to the moon, 238,900 miles away. Not too shabby. Now everyone wants to get to Mars, which averages 140 million miles away. If someone states they are ready to try and only makes it a bit beyond the moon, they "failed" to make Mars, but will have made it farther than any other human to date.

Judgment and comparison round out the primary achievement roadblocks. We have an immense tendency to negatively judge an achievement we truly desire. We think it might be silly or frivolous and will seek to justify it. If we can't justify it, we judge it unworthy and won't try. Here is my counsel: don't justify it. Not to yourself or anyone else. Easy to say, I know. But truly. If you want to try to get on *America's Got Talent* for singing or training hula-hooping cats, just trust the desire. What you gain by trying will add to every aspect of your life.

Comparison is a giant killer, especially in today's culture where everyone's accomplishments are publicized for the world to see. You can't visit a person's social media without seeing their accomplishments, mine included. I'll admit I've had to grapple with this a lot, as every week I am with a guest who is likely younger than I am. They've oftentimes had more going against them in life, but they've had more success than I have had: sometimes more money, more fame, better relationships, and even more joy and fulfillment. I've had to either make peace with it or be overcome by it.

The only way to jump over the roadblocks to achievements is to have courage. You won't get past your fears, so you just have to do it scared.

TAKE ACTION

How many desired achievements have you talked yourself out of? How many times have you justified not trying because it's not reasonable or rational? What are you afraid of, and who are you afraid will see you fail? You won't get past all that fear, so are you going to let it stop you, or just try anyway?

WHAT YOU WANT TO ACHIEVE

Colin O'Brady was a pro triathlete and is now a 10-time world-record-breaking explorer. His feats include the world's first solo, unsupported, and fully human-powered crossing of Antarctica; speed records for the Explorers Grand Slam and the Seven Summits; and the first human-powered ocean row across Drake Passage. During the Covid pandemic, he wrote his second book, *The 12-Hour Walk*, inspired by his Antarctica crossing but also drawing from his ascent of Mt. Everest. A primary premise of the book is Colin asking us, "What is your Everest?" I had Colin on my show in summer 2022 and we started off discussing why we go from being kids with big plans to eventually submitting to the grind and the hope of some fun in the evenings and weekends and a vacation here and there.[5] It's something that happens to most of us. I've thought about it as a father and wondered, if all I show my kids is that adulthood sucks, what do they have to look forward to? I've always bristled at the adult concept of the "glory days"—the notion that we've had some fun in our youth, but after that it's all over, for the most part.

In 2014, after not competing in any sporting events for a while, I entered an off-road duathlon and brought my family along. The race had three loops, and I thought it would be fun to see my kids throughout the race. But when I got there, I couldn't help feeling a little guilty having them all come spend the day just to watch me pass by a few times. But I was so wrong. We still have a video of one of my sons running alongside me as I finished the race, cheering me on. Later, my older kids testified to how inspiring it was to them, to see me doing things that inspired me. It made me remember that during my childhood, I saw my parents pursue things they cared about. And it was one of the greatest gifts, seeing them try and sometimes fail, and no matter the outcome, life went on. It gave me faith to try things and not be devastated if they didn't work out perfectly. The achievements we go after are not just for us—they inspire other people. They give permission to others to try what means something to them.

This is a time to be honest with yourself. To be free. To allow yourself to admit something or some things you'd really like to do. Or just simply try. A favorite quote of mine from a favorite movie, *The Family Stone*, is "You have a freak flag. You just don't fly it." I wish we were sitting together somewhere having coffee or wine and I could tease it out of you. Get out a journal and think and write. Go talk to a friend if you process as you speak. Go for a walk. Go watch *The Secret Life of Walter Mitty* or read *A Million Miles in a Thousand Years*. Maybe go to a concert or sports event or go dancing. Something that gets you out of yourself and thinking bigger and more freely.

Again, don't get hung up on thinking it needs to be some huge endeavor. The point isn't impressing the world but giving life and fulfillment to your soul. But if it is something that seems fairly big to you and is significantly daunting and you are questioning your ability, consider taking some smaller, tangible steps to bolster your confidence. Years ago, I led an organization helping people who wanted to go from traditional employment to self-employment. A big jump, no doubt. In my zeal I found myself advocating the "big idea." The big risk. "Go for it!" I'd say, or "Just Do It!"— recycling worn phrases. And over time I saw it was often too daunting for my audience. Then I noticed some members were achieving some smaller accomplishments, and I saw it gave them the confidence to go after the bigger thing. I started advocating 5K running events. The point wasn't athletics or exercise, but just an easy accomplishment for people to train for and achieve. It doesn't have to be a 5K, but the concept is to find an easier win to prove to yourself you can go after bigger things.

Frans Johansson wrote a book called *The Medici Effect* in 2004, and not long after I heard him speak at an event. What has always stuck with me was his research on entrepreneurs. He somewhat discounted the idea that they were intrinsically more able than other people. He found they were simply willing to try more things than the average person. Don't be average. Just try more things.

TAKE ACTION

What is your Everest? What would inspire you and make you feel proud of yourself? What would you regret not having tried when it's too late to give it a shot? What would you want on your bio or obituary? What would be really cool to add to your résumé or personal profile on a dating site?

WHAT MOTIVATES WHAT YOU WANT TO ACHIEVE

Going back to the movie *Forrest Gump*, you may remember the scene where Forrest proposes marriage to the love of his life, Jenny, but she turns him down. That night they sleep together, and she leaves town the next morning before Forrest wakes up. The scene then picks up with Forrest looking wistfully down the gravel lane of his home. Finally, he stands up, takes a few steps, and breaks into a loping run. Later to a lady on a park bench he recounts, "That day, for no particular reason, I decided to go for a little run." Ultimately, he runs across the entirety of America, turns around, and does it again.

This event happened following the Vietnam War, a time when people were questioning and looking for greater meaning to life. As Forrest continued to run, people took notice. The media gave him attention, and before long groups of people were running along behind them on their own quests. They'd ask advice from Forrest and attach meaning to what he was doing. The questioning of his grand purpose came to a crux as he crossed a bridge surrounded by reporters. They ask him why he is running, and before can respond, pepper him as to whether it's for world peace, the homeless, women's rights, or the environment, or animals. Finally, Forrest blandly answers, "I just felt like running." Back on the park bench as he tells the story to the lady, he says, "They just couldn't believe somebody would do all that running for no particular reason."

I've watched the movie many times by now, and my own estimation is that he ran to medicate his pain of losing Jenny, or having lost his mother, or just to distract himself from the pain of life. Or, maybe he actually was "just running." I guess only the author, Winston Groom, could say. Or maybe he didn't know either.

I offer Forrest's example to help you embrace the achievements you desire, without justification. Which I know sounds nearly impossible. Like the reporters, we want to justify anything we devote ourselves to. When the truth is, the most authentic and pure achievements that truly give us fulfillment are the things we do "for no particular reason." We'll generally craft and communicate a reason, but I find the true motive is an abstract sign that ultimately points to "I just enjoy it." And we often don't know why.

If I look at my own lifetime achievements, whether the ones in my bio or the personal ones I'm most proud of, and ask the question, "Why?," I think the true answer is simply, "Because I wanted to." Why did I want to? "I don't really know." Even my work today, which gives me accolades for podcasting self-help information that people say changes their lives for the better, I mainly do because it's what interests me. I find books and topics and messages I'm curious about and talk about them. How great that it both helps people and I make a good income from it, but it's something I would do regardless. I mentioned a desire to compete for a national mountain bike championship in my age group. Why? Who would be served? How will it help world peace or the economy or the environment? Well, it won't. Then how do I justify all the time I put into the endeavor? Well, I can't. It's my life and I have the desire, and I just no longer have to justify it. That said, let me not discount my responsibilities to my family. I have a really big family, another thing I can't and won't justify. I won't abandon them for a mere interest I want to pursue, and I'm not calling others to shirk their own responsibilities. But I would have you question what your responsibilities truly are, and to whom, as more often than not we let unnecessary "responsibilities" be our excuse for playing small. And while we do have a responsibility to others, I find that giving priority to the pursuit of achievements we're proud of makes us better, more joyful humans. And that serves everyone in our lives.

Think about it like this: Maybe there's an unpopular food or food combination you like, perhaps it's peanut butter and pickle sandwiches. If I ask you why on earth you like that mix, you'll likely say, "Because it tastes great!" Which is a false statement, since taste is not an objective reality, only a perspective. The only true answer would be, "I have no idea, but it gives my taste buds great joy, and I'm going to eat it as often as possible. So be it." You have permission to look at your desired achievements in the same fashion.

Gary Barkalow is an author, speaker, and old friend of mine. In his book *It's Your Call*, he gives great attention to trusting the true desires of your heart.[6] Not the fleeting, passing desires, but the abiding, deep-seated desires that stick with us. The childhood desire that still exists. The answer to, "I've always wanted to/been interested in _____." Though if you have a seismic moment and for the first time get hit with a vision of something you know you have to do, don't discount it either. Don't minimize these desires.

Elevate them. The full meanings of your desired pursuits may be elusive to you, and that's OK. Be prepared to answer someone's question of, "So why did you do that?" with, "I don't know, I just really wanted to, and for some reason it feels great." Enough said.

TAKE ACTION

What desires have you discounted because you couldn't fully justify them? What pursuits do you enjoy that simply make you feel good and inspire you?

SEE YOURSELF THERE

A recent Harvard study focused on the question of whether we as humans tend to think more in words or pictures. Elinor Amit, an affiliate of Harvard's Psychology Department, and Evelina Fedorenko of Harvard Medical School led the study and found that even when people were told to use verbal thinking, they still created visual images to go along with their inner speech.[7] If we look at social media today, it's easy to make a case that we are most inclined toward pictures and visual images.

To see ourselves as having achieved something in the future is incredibly difficult. We can vividly recall past achievements, of course, as they are often imprinted in our minds, and today we generally have an actual photo of the experience. But to take who and where you are today and see yourself as having accomplished a brand-new achievement is admittedly elusive.

The person you will be when you achieve your heart's desire doesn't currently exist. That person is the future you, and you don't have a literal picture you can pull up and peruse. Even when we think we can envision the future, it's often based on realities of the past. I think I can already see this coming Christmas, but all I'm doing is revisiting the poignant Christmas scenes of last year and the decades before. To truly see a picture of something in the future is difficult. But regarding achievements we can use some substitutes.

You can not only see in pictures, but also in video: people crossing the line from marathons and triathlons and any number of athletic pursuits. You can see people graduating from college. People losing 100 pounds. People learning to play a musical instrument and doing their first recital. Whatever the achievements you have in mind, you can find a wealth of visuals of other people striving for and achieving them. And among all those pictures and videos you'll likely find someone you relate to. Someone who looks like you, feels like you, and acts like you. Someone you can connect to, even in an anonymous picture. Use this. Cut it out, paste it, and copy it somewhere and superimpose your own image over it. If you're a Photoshop whiz, maybe you can literally do this.

As of this writing, I don't have a picture of myself at a table stacked high with the book you are now reading, pen in hand and smiling as I sign books for people. But I've seen hundreds of these pictures from people on my show. People I have gotten to know and relate to, and the mental image of me at the table is now easy to conjure up. I've become familiar with it. You can likewise become a veritable connoisseur of images of people achieving your desired pursuit. If you implant the image in your head enough times, you'll likely find yourself subconsciously supplanting your own face in there, even having vivid dreams of the sort.

Do the work to see your future self emerging and then picture yourself working toward and arriving at your desired achievements. Make the imagery part of your current world. Like a detective tacking up evidence on a wall, use these images to study, contemplate, and consider until all the pieces come together to reveal an outcome.

TAKE ACTION

Where can you find imagery of people beginning, working toward, and arriving at the accomplishments you desire? How and where can you surround yourself with this imagery and begin implanting it into your mental reality?

YOUR ACHIEVEMENT ZONE

The best example I can give for pursuit of and benefit from successfully finding an influencing zone of achievement is one I experienced firsthand. I mentioned that my father's parents were born into Amish families. My father grew up on a farm living a near-Amish existence. Yet even in his small town in Ohio he was exposed to people who lived a different life—one with more freedom and abundance than he'd experienced in his home. He became aware that he desired a different lifestyle than what he was living. After finishing high school, he left his home, which was very hard to do in a culture where you are expected to work the family farm until you take it over. From there, he enrolled in Ohio State University, where he got a degree in psychology. He immersed himself in an entirely different world of philosophy, theology, psychology, and self-help. He's never stopped nor looked back. He surrounded himself by the types of minds and lifestyles he wanted to emulate.

When times were good, he immersed himself in the teachings, products, seminars, and events of the people he wanted to emulate. When times were bad and he was working to avoid bankruptcy (which he did!), he immersed himself *even more* in the teachings, products, seminars, and events of the people he wanted to emulate. Even as he became "Dan Miller, bestselling author of *48 Days to the Work You Love*" and a beloved career, business, and life coach and mentor to thousands, he continues to surround himself with the people and influences he wants to emulate.

Thanks to my father, as a child, I knew the works and words of Dale Carnegie, Brian Tracy, and Zig Ziglar better than many adults do. I also grew up with no better example of what we can do in order to pursue and realize the achievements we most desire.

I share this story because it shows the importance of finding others who have achieved or are in the pursuit of achieving the same kind of goals you are pursuing and adopting them as your family. While I was lucky enough to have someone like this in my actual family, my father didn't, which is why he went out to surround himself with people who were just like the person he wanted to be. Do the same for yourself. Become as fluent, actually more fluent, in their world. Pay expert coaches and consultants to give you immediate immersion. If that isn't in the cards for you right now, dive into all the books and content you can read. Subscribe to podcasts and newsletters of people you admire and aim to be like. Immerse yourself in any way you can.

The quickest way to what we want to achieve is by being surrounded and learning from the people who have achieved it. They are there for you to journey with. Go drive with them.

> ### TAKE ACTION
>
> Where can you find groups who are going after your desired achievements? Whom do you know, and whom do they know?

CHAPTER SUMMARY

▶ **Case for Achievements:** We define ourselves mostly by what we have done. The number one deathbed regret is about the dreams we didn't fulfill. Dreams are at the core, as are our accomplishments. We want to do things that make us proud of ourselves. As we mature, our greatest regrets will be the things we didn't try and pursue. We have the opportunity to deny those regrets by going after what we value, right now, before it's too late.

▶ **What Is Inherent:** The achievements of your ancestors can serve to boost your confidence, possibly pointing you toward a particular talent, or to taking certain actions.

▶ **What You've Been Exposed To:** The achievements of those closest to you give you permission to strive for your own great achievements. The more you are aware of the achievements of those you are connected to, the more confidence you'll have in similar feats.

▶ **Roadblocks to Avoid:** We are "smart enough to know better" and see the obstacles to doing something truly great, so we tend not to try, while those who are "dumb enough not to know better" just go do it. We know we're not better than everyone else, but we can each be better in certain areas and do great things. Yet we fear going after our greatness because it makes us accountable to doing more. We tend to minimize our efforts by judging their merit and comparing ourselves to others who have done more. We'll never get rid of our fears. But we can only go forward with courage.

▶ **What You Authentically Want:** Don't think the glory days are behind you. What a sad story to tell yourself. Remember that what you try to achieve is greater than the sum of the achievement; it will inspire others and give them permission to try things as well. Your achievement is not big or small, it's just what you desire. You don't have to justify it. Just be free and give yourself permission to explore new horizons.

▶ **What Motivates You:** You don't have to justify your "why" to anyone—or even yourself. This is often a handicapping trap. You can just run, like Forrest Gump. Or enjoy peanut butter and pickle sandwiches. Whether it's a fairly long-standing desire, or one that hits you in a deep way for the first time, give it strong consideration and watch out for "analysis paralysis."

PART THREE

VICTORY LAP

CHAPTER 10

Driving Mastery

Now that we've walked through the key areas of life and you've considered what you want and why, this is a bonus section and exercise to help you really conceptualize being driven and being in control of your life.

Most people hop in their vehicle, shift to drive, and go. Or at least in the United States, where the norm is to drive cars with automatic transmissions. The only conscious decision we make is whether to accelerate and brake. Or take a drink, as the average American car now boasts 2.5 cup holders for every passenger. But professional drivers have a completely different experience when driving. They shift manually to speed up, and they shift manually to slow down. They are fully aware of every nuance, and as such, are able to travel at a far greater speed than any of us mere mortals. Not to mention they aren't drinking the entire time . . .

This chapter is a pro session in switching you from automatic to manual in your daily tasks. From mindless and reactive living to mindful and proactive living. Yes, it can be challenging and counterintuitive at first, just like making the change from automatic to manual shifting. With less drinking. But this shift can harness a power you are likely missing—the power to reframe your reality.

When I was growing up, my parents would often respond to negative events by asking, "What does this make possible?" That question has stayed with me, because the inherent lesson was that we can take any trauma and allow it to cripple us, or we can realize the opportunity for gaining insight and wisdom. The former choice makes us weaker; the latter makes us stronger, and we get to choose. The difference is absolutely everything. It truly is all about perspective.

I can't overstate the power of this one habit I've found that creates a massively life-altering paradigm shift in your mind. It's a simple yet profound practice of replacing one word with another, which forces our minds to run on a different and life-giving operating system.

Stop saying you *have to*. Start saying you *want to*. To everything.

This single change in word choice will reprogram your mind and forever alter your very character. It requires ownership of your actions. When each and every action of your life is by choice instead of requirement, your perspective is turned from upside down to right side up. This is incredibly simple in theory, yet proves extremely difficult to carry out in everyday life. It's like taking your dominant hand and tying it behind you all day, forcing you to use your other hand for everything. To switch from *having* to do everything to *wanting* to is challenging, but if you make it a habit, I promise it will blow your mind. The result is you become CEO of your life.

My kids are required to do daily chores in the home, such as cleaning dishes and putting food away after meals. What kid ever actually wants to do this? While I appreciate that they often do it without complaining, they still do it out of obligation and would not do it otherwise. They are not, in fact, CEOs of their lives. They can rightly say, "I have to do the dishes."

Yet lo and behold, the fateful day will come when they move out of the family home and into their own place. The first night they make dinner on their own, and onward, they will wash the dishes because they want to. It is their choice. Even if they take liberty to leave them dirty for a day or two, at some point they will want to clean them because they do not want dirty dishes that smell and grow mold. But again, it is now their choice, and choice is a game changer.

If we evaluate common words in our culture, you would be surprised to learn how often we speak of what we "have to" do. It's as common and subconscious as walking by someone and benignly saying, "How ya' doing?" We are not actually asking; it's just saying hi. But if the person were to actually respond in earnest and start telling you, intimately, how they are doing, you would likely soon interject with something you "have to" do to get away as soon as possible.

In truth you do not *have* to do anything. But you sincerely *want* to remove yourself from this obligatory conversation. Can you imagine saying the truth? "Hey, so sorry, but I really want to get on with my day. Bye!" Instead, we say it in a way that removes our personal culpability, "Hey, I've gotta run, pick my kids up/get to work/rescue a kitten up a tree."

This has bled over into a cultural norm. Nearly everything we do is stated as a *have to* or *got to*. We are all apparently victims of life, led by things we have no control over. And it shapes our mindset into one of victimhood and powerlessness. Instead, imagine living for just a day, only stating things as what you *want*.

"OK, I want to get to the office now!"

"I want to go pick my kids up from school."

"I want to talk to Frank about the problem we are having with customer service."

"I want to grab some groceries before heading home."

Friends, I assure you, this is a radical shift in your overall outlook on life at large. You will initially find it is nearly impossible and fairly uncomfortable and cumbersome, as you can't actually lead with stating "I want" without considering if or why you really do. What will surface is awareness of how habitually you speak as a victim to your life and are dishonest with others and yourself about your true thoughts and feelings.

Have to, *got to*, and *need to* are the words of victims. Imagine having vast wealth and power beyond measure. What would you then ever *have* to do? You would do whatever you darn well pleased. But we speak as if we are indentured servants of life. Beggars, even.

This is a life-changing practice, and you won't get it right all the time. Here's an example of my own struggle with this shift: Recently I was at my office on an early Saturday morning, and I got a text from my wife asking if I'm OK. I texted back that I woke up at five o'clock with things on my mind and came in to get some work done. I rarely ever work on the weekends, but we were leaving for a long trip to Florida in a few days. I had just launched some initiatives, and I knew the work wouldn't do itself.

My fingers instinctually typed out, "I just have to get work done before we leave." In the back of my mind, my hope was that my wife would respond with, "Oh honey, I'm so sorry. Thank you for all you do to provide for our family," and so on and so forth. Aww, isn't that sweet. I play the victim, she strokes my ego, and I feel validated in my big outpouring of efforts . . .

But that's a false reality, or at least a weak one. I work for myself. I'm not financially destitute. I'm my own boss and create my own workload. I could do less and earn less and have less. Or in this case, nobody would die and the negative consequences would be relatively few, if any, if I did not work that morning. But I want more, so I do more. Furthermore, I chose to go on a vacation to the beach with my family. Poor me! Nobody forced me. So that conscious choice necessitates that I do extra work leading up to it, if I want to keep things at a level I want. I can so often get this Superman complex that inflates my importance in the world.

I do not mean to minimize critical junctures in your life, or mine. Sometimes we are, in fact, victimized. My wife recently suffered an injury that found us at the ER at 3 a.m. That's a credible "I have to get my wife to the hospital!" instance. However, if push came to shove in this particular case, I bet she could have driven herself. Or I have a working phone that can dial 911 and I can have an ambulance sent out. But I did not *want* either of those options. I *wanted* to take care of her. My choice.

Think about your daily life. Start with going to your office or place of employment. If you are an employee, do you really have to? Do you truly have no choice in the matter? I promise it is more than semantics to state you *want* to go to the office. If you do not love or at least enjoy your work, then you must at least appreciate getting paid. So, at the least, state that fact out loud, "I *want* to get to the office because I value my job that provides a paycheck, which affords me my lifestyle." Boom, now you are in control. You retain your power. You are responsible. You do what you do by choice. You are empowered.

Another example is the task of picking up the kids. Let's say you are actively engaged in work that you appreciate and it pays the bills, but your kids are done with school. You *have to* go get them or they will be abandoned, right?

Otherwise, social services will swoop in and find them some actual responsible parents elsewhere. Just think of the mindset, though. You can't say, "I have to go pick up my kids" without triggering something in your mind that makes it feel like a burden and summons pity from those in your proximity. Picture the mom or dad who says it. They don't say it with joy, but with an eyeroll or hint of exasperation. But change it to, "All right, well, now I want to go pick up my kids!" Literally try speaking those two different statements out loud. When you say, "have to," the word "kids" at the end is said with a downward intonation. But change it to "want to," and you'll likely say "kids" with an upturned intonation. Just stating the word *want* naturally adjusts our attitude. This is legit cognitive training right here, friends.

The power of *want* cannot be overstated. It rewires our brains. And ultimately, it is more honest. For most anyone reading this book, the vast majority of your life today is where you are by choice. With all due respect, and pointing the finger at myself, there is very little negative in my lifetime that ultimately was not a result of something I wanted and chose to do. My wife and I never planned to have seven biological kids, but we actively participated in the causation. None of my business ordeals happened as a result of endeavors I was forced to pursue. I went in with great confidence, gusto, and desire. I put myself in that place and made the majority of all decisions along the way.

It's a worthy endeavor to see your current circumstances through the prism of personal choice. Take it as a task. I challenge you to claim that everything you have in life today, every aspect of your circumstances, you came to by choice. Even if you were victimized along the way, how did you choose to respond that resulted in where you are today?

Friends, this is possibly the most liberating action you can take in your life, as it frees you and empowers you, regardless of your circumstances. Many of which you can't control. You can't control the external, but you can control the internal.

I know people who never place blame anywhere but only choose to change their paradigm in having made choices that resulted in all their current circumstances . . . and it was mind-blowing. It doesn't mean they don't feel negative emotions. I've tried that most of my life, and it doesn't end well. Today I strive to acknowledge the disappointments and really feel them. But I vow not to let them run my life.

Even in the little things of daily life. How many times per day does the average person say, "I've got to get some breakfast/lunch/dinner/food"? Few people in developed nations know what actual hunger is. We are led by appetite, addiction, and the mere habit of eating. I'm convinced food is the number one drug on planet Earth, and we are all addicted. But an easy way to lose a few pounds is to take this *want* challenge, as you will find just saying, "I want to eat lunch" will often serve as a reminder you are in no way, shape, or form, actually hungry. Yes, you *want* to eat because you are accustomed to putting something in your mouth at a particular time of day. You mainly want the hit of dopamine as you see food, taste food, and fill your belly. Hey, me too. But fessing up to the truth will result in taking in less overall food and calories and not making excuses for it. Just own it.

The term "extreme ownership" has become a buzzword. Top podcaster, author, and former Navy Seal Jocko Willink wrote a book with that as the title. His point was what I'm getting to here, with the same flavor as Tom Bilyeu's message of "It's All Your Fault" I shared previously. We don't like taking ownership of hard things because two words generally go along with them: *fault* and *blame* We'll go to herculean efforts to never let those words be placed on us. I believe we'd do better to be OK with them.

As mentioned previously, I live in a national forest. We've been evacuated a number of times because of forest fires. If next week a forest fire comes through and burns my house down, I'm willing to accept it's my fault. I'm to blame. Or at least, I take responsibility. I don't have to live there. I know the danger. I could sell my house in a week and move to the desert with not a tree in sight and no possibility of a forest fire. But I'm not going to do that. I pay for home insurance, and I take the risk by staying where I am. That feels so much better, and it will feel better if my home burns down, because I've already prepared myself for the possibility and my chance of recovery is far higher in taking ownership of the risk.

Now let's think about the little benign things we say that not only rob us of our ownership, but are, in truth, lies. "Little white lies" that we think don't hurt anyone. But they hurt us. I'm not talking from some religious or "holier than thou" perspective. I'm simply acknowledging the harm we do to our ability to be authentic when we give away our responsibility and power.

In our moment-to-moment life we use the "have to" mentality to be dishonest, and it is not benign. If I'm at my kid's soccer game and end up chitchatting with someone, which is not my favorite thing to do, I'm likely to take a deep breath, glance at my watch, and say, "Wow, look at the time. I've gotta get going!" Which suggests I have family waiting on me or an appointment to get to or something that I just respond to because I'm not in control. This is wholly socially acceptable, but it's untrue. I simply *want* to stop chitchatting and do something I enjoy more. That's it. But I play the victim to this person and myself. And what's odd is that the other person, subconsciously at least, knows what I'm doing. They do the same thing—we all accept each other's white lies and victim speech.

Though I realize, wouldn't it feel odd to state the truth? To say, "Hey, I want to stop talking with you now, so see you later," and walk away? Yeah, I can't really see myself doing that. But I can say, even with the sigh and look at my watch, "Hey, I'm gonna run, really good to see you!" That is not offensive, and I retain ownership.

In episode 763 of *The Ziglar Show* I talked with Will Bowen, author of a book titled *A Complaint Free World*.[1] He started an initiative with a purple bracelet, and the point was not to complain. About anything. And if you do, you switch the bracelet to your other wrist. The goal is to go as long as possible keeping it on one wrist, as you don't complain.

This is a very similar effort. Heck, use a bracelet if you want. Erase the offending and damaging word *have to* from your vernacular. I know it's actually two words, but we say them together so often I think of them as one. It makes it easier if you share the objective with those you are around. Share this message so you can self-correct in front of them when you slip up. You may find them considering and adopting the initiative as well. I honestly think of it in my own mind in reference to Terry Real's book *Us*, where in Chapter 1 he describes the Adaptive Child and Wise Adult. I feel like the Wise Adult when I own what I'm going to do or what I did.

Please hear me. This is not a cute little self-help exercise. It's life-changing. Most of us have no idea how much of ourselves we have minimized and handicapped by adopting this victim language. This one change in your vocabulary can increase your peace and joy and gratitude for life. You no longer *have* to do anything. You don't *need* to do anything. You *want* to. You are going to, of your own volition.

Have fun with it. It's helpful to make a list. Let me help with some paradigm shifters:

- ▶ "I want to get up now!" When the alarm clock goes off. Why do you want to? Because you want to have some centering time before the family wakes up or you start your workday. Because you want to take your kids to school, as not doing so would result in consequences you, again, don't *want* to have! Because in truth, you could choose to let them stay home. If that means you can't go to work because they are young children, you can choose that too. If you would get fired, you could choose that too. You do not *want* to get fired because you want to get paid. It's all from what you *want*.

- ▶ "I want to exercise" because I want to look and feel and perform well. It's all for me!

- ▶ "I want to skip eating this morning (or this day)" because it's good to give my body a break, it will benefit me and my life!

- ▶ "I want to have a hard talk with my spouse/kid," or even if you again just say, "I'm going to." You don't have to, but the truth is you want to because the consequences of not doing it are more than you want to bear. Own it.

- ▶ "I want to go grab some lunch." Your body probably does not need it from a physiological sense, but your taste buds want it and it gives you joy. Own it. Admit it!

You get the idea. Will Bowen has the "no complaint challenge." Shaunti Feldhahn, a favorite author of mine whom I cite so often, has a book titled *The Kindness Challenge: Thirty Days to Improve Any Relationship* where you say nothing negative, and proactively say positives about someone for 30 days. Both challenges are, again, life-changing.

So I'm tempted to tell you to take the "want challenge" for even a day. Try one day, but make sure it's a day you are around people and conversing, where you have plenty of opportunity to errantly claim you *have to* do so many things.

But I truly feel "challenge" minimizes the true gravity of the issue. It's more like a "right." It is your right and privilege to claim responsibility and ownership of your actions, and therefore your life. We are a culture very much obsessed with our personal rights, but they are most often claimed within the context of victimhood—we often think an outside force is infringing on our ability to do what we want to do. This is not that. This is your right and privilege to be whole. In taking every action of my day and week and month and year and life, and then viewing and owning it as a want, I claim my right to be whole. To be happy. To be full so I can pour out to and serve others. My family doesn't want a husband and father who *has to* take care of and provide for them. They want one who *wants* to. Your employer doesn't want an employee who *has to* come to work and *has to* do their duties, they want one who *wants* to. Your customers don't want to buy your product or service because you *have to* sell it in order to make a buck. They want to buy your product or service because you *want* them to benefit from it. Your friends and associates don't want you dismissing yourself from them because you are a victim to untold things and *have to* go. They want you inspired and vibrant and involved in activities you desire and choose to pursue.

You pull yourself down and you pull everyone around you down when you *have to* do anything. You pull yourself up and add to your and everyone's life when you *want* to do everything.

So here's to you, and everything you want to do today, and in your driven life!

ACKNOWLEDGMENTS

King Solomon in the Bible claimed, "There is nothing new under the sun." This has always been profound to me in the world of authoring and influence as people continually claim the next "secret" and new thing. While I believe we are capable of truly authentic thoughts and ideas, any educated person will have the voices and perspectives of all the people responsible for everything they've learned conjoined to any concept they birth. At best I take credit for constructing some fresh insights into more understandable perspectives well fitting for the unique evolution of time we find ourselves in.

Thus to credit all the sources accounting for the ideas of this book is monumentally overwhelming and daunting, as it would take a book of equal length to list all the individuals whose brains and hearts I ride on the backs of.

To all of you who have influenced my life overall . . . thank you. Bless you. You deserve more credit than anyone. If you've ever known me for a time, I'd just adore hearing from you to tell you what you meant, and mean, to me: kmiller@kevinmiller.co.

I will however, hit some highlight credits related to this book specifically:

My Family: I learned more about my drive from you than anyone else, and you benefited and suffered from it most: Teri, Breanne, Caleb, Autumn, Eliza, Ian, Canyon, Serene, Nekoda, Jaydaria, and then Mason, Andre, Fabian, and Reina.

My Parents, Dan and Joanne Miller: You got me started on this journey and ignited my drive.

Tom Ziglar: Your friendship, the Ziglar family, the legacy of your dad, and the Ziglar platform are massive parts of why this book exists.

Randy James: The past decade of my life has been massively shaped by you. You drive . . . so well.

Scott, Todd, Dustin, Ronnie, and Jared: Words can't express. Thanks for sharing your journeys and helping me with mine.

The over 200 guests who have given me their time and heart on the podcasts. Your specific influence and the sharing of your journey is the heartbeat of this book. Living inspired lives from your clarified values is what I most hope is imparted to the reader.

Jennifer Kasius at Kevin Anderson & Associates: Your insight not only brought the book together, but you helped me find my groove in the project.

Thanks to Park & Fine and McGraw Hill for taking a chance on a guy who had some podcast listeners.

Thanks to the Stearmans, Adams, and Logsdons for use of their homes for my writing getaways.

My Driven To Live community, thanks for walking and talking with me.

Special recognition to everyone involved in Trinity Sports Group and Free Agent Academy. You loved and served and tolerated me at times when I was driving with the pedal floored and my eyes shut. I wish I could give each of you a hug and an apology. Thank you from the bottom of my heart.

NOTES

CHAPTER 2

1. Bruce Selcraig, "The Real Robinson Crusoe," *Smithsonian Magazine*, July 2005, https://www.smithsonianmag.com/history/the-real-robinson-crusoe-74877644/.
2. Sheena Iyengar and Mark Leeper, "When Choice Is Demotivating: Can One Desire Too Much of a Good Thing?," *Journal of Personality and Social Psychology* 79, no. 6 (200): 995–1006.
3. Sonja Lyubomirsky, "What Determines Happiness" (pie chart).
4. Ryan Pace, *Dark Psychology and Gaslighting Manipulation* (independently published, 2020).
5. Ray Ward, "Victor Serebriakoff: Ex-manual Worker Who Rose to the Top in Mensa," Obituary, *The Guardian*, January 5, 2000, https://www.theguardian.com/news/2000/jan/06/guardianobituaries2.

CHAPTER 3

1. Rabbi Daniel and Susan Lapin, "Teenage Depression," Rabbi Daniel Lapin, https://rabbidaniellapin.com/teenage-depression/.

2. "Attending Church Is the Key to Good Mental Health," The London School of Economics and Political Science, *LSE Health News,* 2015, https://www.lse.ac.uk/lse-health /news-events/2015/church-key-to-good-mental-health.

3. https://www.youtube.com/shorts/UZ3p4uya3so.

CHAPTER 4

1. Tahira Sequeira, "Nearly One in Three Finns Suffering from Loneliness," *Helsinki Times,* February 10, 2021, https://www.helsinkitimes.fi/finland/news-in -brief/18681-nearly-one-in-three-finns-suffering-from -loneliness.html.

2. Jussi Tanskanen and Timo Anttila, "A Prospective Study of Social Isolation, Loneliness, and Mortality in Finland," *American Journal of Public Health,* November 2016, https://ajph.aphapublications.org/doi/10.2105 /AJPH.2016.303431.

CHAPTER 6

1. Terrence Real, *Us: Getting Past You and Me to Build a More Loving Relationship* (Goop Press, 2022), 76–77. Used with permission.

CHAPTER 7

1. Thomas C. Corley, "The More People Love Their Jobs, the Quicker They Get Rich," *Insider,* August 14, 2015, https://www.businessinsider.com/people-who-love-their -jobs-get-richer-2015-8.

CHAPTER 8

1. Financial Security Program and Dyvonne Body, "The Burden of Debt on Mental and Physical Health," Aspen Institute, August 2, 2018, https://www.aspeninstitute .org/blog-posts/hidden-costs-of-consumer-debt/.

CHAPTER 9

1. Bronnie Ware, *The Top Five Regrets of the Dying: A Life Transformed by the Dearly Departing* (Hay House, 2012), 44.
2. "How to Leverage Our Regrets: Dan Pink," *Self Helpful with Kevin Miller* (podcast), #969, https://podcasts .apple.com/us/podcast/how-to-leverage-our-regrets-dan -pink/id192820274?i=1000551747653.
3. Daniel H. Pink, *The Power of Regret: How Looking Backward Helps Us Move Forward* (Riverhead Books, 2022), 15.
4. Quote Investigator, "Our Deepest Fear Is Not That We Are Inadequate. Our Deepest Fear Is That We Are Powerful Beyond Measure," https://quoteinvestigator.com /2019/06/30/deepest/.
5. "Reboot and Upgrade Your Mind and Capacity: Record Breaking Explorer Colin O'Brady Part 1," *Self Helpful with Kevin Miller* (podcast), https://podcasts.apple.com /fr/podcast/reboot-upgrade-your-mind-capacity-record -breaking-explorer/id192820274?i=1000571319515.
6. Gary Barkalow, *It's Your Call: What Are You Doing Here?* (The Noble Heart, 2021).
7. Peter Reuell, "The Power of Picturing Thoughts," *Harvard Gazette*, May 11, 2017, https://news.harvard .edu/gazette/story/2017/05/visual-images-often-intrude -on-verbal-thinking-study-says/.

CHAPTER 10

1. "Complaining is poisoning our success, with Will Bowen" Self Helpful with Kevin Miller (podcast), https://podcasts.apple.com/us/podcast/763-complaining -is-poisoning-our-success-with-will-bowen/id192820274 ?i=1000467222481

INDEX

Abilities, belief in, 130–132
Abundance mentality, 184
Accountability, 62, 116, 149, 211
Achievement, xi–xii, 201–224
    authentic desires for, 213–216
    environmental factors in, 208–210
    envisioning, 38–39, 219–221
    genetic factors in, 205–208
    genetic propensity for, 27
    mental roadblocks to, 210–213
    motives for, 36, 216–219
    personal value of, 202–205
    supportive zone for, 221–223
Adaptive Child, 147–148, 235
Adoption, 57–58
Advertising, 193–194
Advice, asking for, 173–174
Affinity groups, 87–88
Affirmation, 86
Affluent social groups, 187–188
Africa, 57, 60
Agreement with motives, 8, 15–16, 61
Alcoholics Anonymous, 116
Alone (TV series), 178
Altruism, 36
Ambivalence, 85, 183
American Public Health Association, 72
Amish church, 30–31, 53, 221
Amit, Eleanor, 219
Animals, health span for, 120–121
Antarctica, crossing of, 213–214
Anti-Sparktype, 33
Anxiety, 178, 184, 207
Appearance (*see* Physical health and appearance)

Appetite, 114
Appreciation, 179–180, 194
Art, as motive, 192–194
Asch, Solomon, 39
Aspen Institute, 179
Association of possessions, 193–194
Athletics, 163–164, 203–204
Atlas of the Heart (Brown), 34
Attractiveness, 121–123
Authentic desire(s), xiii
    for achievement, 213–216
    and beliefs, 37–38
    financial decisions driven by, 189–191
    to find purpose, 59–60
    giving attention to, 218–219
    to improve physical health, 102
    for mental and emotional state, 143–145
    for physical health, 118–121
    in proactive living, 234–235
    in relationships, 81–83, 90–91
    in unique drive, 30–34
    vocational decisions driven by, 166–168
Authority figures, 139–140, 159–160 (*See also specific types*)
Autobiographies, 68
Autonomy, 89–90, 160
Avendano, Mauricio, 51
Awareness, 8, 11, 26–27
Awareness (Mello), 61–62

Bangladesh, 107
Barkalow, Gary, 218–219

Beliefs:
about drive, 3–19
and capacity for performance, 130–134
as component of unique drive, 36–37
conviction and, 65–66
unhelpful (*see* Mental roadblocks)
(*See also* Envisioning change)
Belonging, 39–41, 51, 116, 186–187
Berra, Yogi and Carmen, xi–xii
Best, doing our, 130–131
Bilyeu, Tom, 55–56, 233
Biographies, 68
Birth order, 76
The Birth Order Book (Leman), 76
Bitterness, about money, 185
Blame, 55, 56, 233–234
The Blue Zones (Buettner), 67, 116
Body:
care and maintenance of, 104–105, 123
mind and, 105
(*See also* Physical health and appearance)
Bogues, Muggsy, 24, 28
Boldness Regrets, 201–202
Boundaries, setting, xii
Bowen, Will, 235, 236
Brain, 52, 207, 232
Brainwashing, 28–29
"Brain-washing Tactics Force Chinese into Ranks of Communist Party" (Hunter), 28
Brown, Brené, 34
Bruce Banner (the Hulk), 16
The Bucket List (film), 204
Bucket lists, 204
Buechner, Frederick, 12, 48, 49
Buettner, Dan, 67, 116
Burnout, xi, xii, 165
Business owners (*see* Entrepreneurs)

Candid Camera (TV show), 39
Caregivers:
financial decision-making by, 182–183
health and wellness of, 110–111
mental/emotional state of, 138–140
value of relationships for, 74–78
view of purpose by, 53–54
vocational decisions of, 159–162
Carnegie, Dale, 222
Celebrity couples, 94–95
Challenge, proactive living, 235–237
Challenging times, relationships during, 77–78

Chambers of Commerce, 87
Change (*see* Envisioning change)
Child-free couples, 84, 92–93
Children:
activity levels of, 110
confidence and achievements for, 206, 214
emotional adaptation by, 147–148
instilling drive in, xi, 9
parents' influence on, 28–30
personal choice for, 228–229
physical activity and diet for, 117
proactive mindset about caring for, 231–232
relationships between parents and, 83–84, 92–93, 97–98
vocational expectations on, 162–164
Chronic illness, 67, 72, 103
Circumstances, personal choice and, 232–233
Clear, James, 12
Coaching, 126–127, 149, 222
Codependent relationships, 91–92
Cognitive dissonance, 195
Cognitive predispositions, 136–137
Collaboration, 88–90
Collins, Francis, 75, 106, 108
Commitment, 40, 64–66
Community, 79, 116, 149
Comparison, 186–187, 212–213
Compensation, 179–180, 190, 193
Completeness, 91–93
Conferences, 198
Confidence, 204, 206–207, 215
Conflict, 9–10
Conformity, 30, 34, 39–41, 117
Connections, 198
Control, 58, 141–143, 184
Conventions, 198
Conviction, 65–67, 172
Counseling, 97, 149
Covey, Stephen, 6
Covid-19 pandemic, 72, 79
Coworkers, 40, 88–90, 117–118
Credibility, 188, 205
CrossFit, 116
Crow, Sheryl, 204
Cultural norms, 80, 82, 91, 116–117, 143–144, 229–230
Curves, 116

Danger, misidentifying, 138
Defoe, Daniel, 22
Denver, John, 32
Deprivation mindset, 113–115

Desire, as motivator, 8, 9, 36 (*See also* Authentic desire(s))
Diabetes, 106
Diet, 107, 111–115, 117–118
Dietitians, 126–127
Difficult conversations, 236
Dilbert (cartoon), 160
Disappointment, 233
DISC personality profile, 33
Discipline, 112, 115
Discomfort, 102–103, 116, 196, 204
Diseases of despair, 73, 103
Dissatisfaction, 102–103
Divorce, 122
Documentaries, 68
Dopamine, 103, 233
Downton Abbey (TV series), 181
Drake & Josh (TV series), 125
Dread, 115
Drive:
    beliefs about, 3–19
    building, 16–17
    defined, ix, xiii
    uneven, 5
    universal capacity for, xiii–xiv, 27–28
Drug addicts, 13
Duhigg, Charles, 12

Ebenezer Scrooge, 156
Education system, 163
Ego, 61, 62, 146
Emory University, 135
Emotional state (*see* Mental and emotional state)
Emotional transference, 135–136
Emotions:
    about money, 180–181, 194
    about physical health and wellness, 113
    and beliefs, 38, 39
    as motives, 34–36, 63, 94
    (*See also* Feelings)
Energy, in friendships, 86
Enjoyment, 115, 185, 214–218
Enneagram personality profile, 33
Entrepreneurs:
    achievements for, 215
    exposure to, 31, 34, 149, 160, 162
    mental/emotional state of, 145–146
    purpose for, 55
    social groups for, 88, 149
    vocational decisions of, 160, 162
Environmental factors:
    in achievement, 208–210
    in financial decision-making, 182–186
    in health of relationships, 77–78
    in mental and emotional state, 138–141
    in physical health, 108–112
    in pursuit of purpose, 53–54
    in unique drive, 28–30
    in vocational decision-making, 159–162
Envisioning change:
    achievement-related, 38–39, 219–221
    in financial decision-making, 195–197
    in mental and emotional state, 147–148
    in physical health, 124–125
    in pursuit of purpose, 64–67
    in relationships, 94–96
    in vocational decision-making, 168–172
Epigenetic inheritance, 135–136
Erasmus University Medical Center, 51
Erhard, Werner, 32
The Everyday Hero Manifesto (Sharma), 80
Exercise, 110–111, 113, 115, 127, 236
Expectations:
    about physical health, 104, 124
    about vocation, 160, 162–164
    and financial decisions, 186–187
    as part of environment, 30
    and performance, 131–132
    relational, 77–80, 84, 87–88, 90
    as roadblock to change, 40–41
Extended family, 77, 84–85, 139, 159
Extreme ownership, 233–234

Failure, 209–210, 212
Faith, 46–50, 53, 64, 137, 139, 184
Family:
    achievements of, 205–206, 208–209
    devotion to, 54
    financial decisions of, 181–182, 185–186
    and mental/emotional state, 135–137
    and physical health, 109–112, 116–118
    relationships within, 74–76, 84–85
    social pressure from, 40
    vocational decisions by, 157–158, 162–163
Family legacy, 207
The Family Stone (film), 214–215
Fault, 233–234
Fear, 36, 135–137, 179, 184, 211
Fedorenko, Evelina, 219

Feelings:
  about family, 85
  about vocation, 155–158, 169–170
  (*See also* Emotions)
Feldhahn, Shaunti, 236
Fields, Jonathan, 33, 90
Financial decisions, 177–200
  authentic desires as driver of, 189–191
  environmental influences on, 182–186
  envisioning better, 38–39, 195–197
  genetic influences on, 181–182
  and meaning of money, 177–181
  mental roadblocks in, 186–189
  motives for making, 35, 192–194
  supportive zone for, 197–199
  vocational and, 165, 166, 169–170, 190
Financial environments, other, 197–198
Financial Peace (Ramsey), 177
Finland, 71–72
"Follow My Feet" (song), 55
Food Rules (Pollan), 114
Ford, Henry, 154
Forgiveness, 140, 148
Forrest Gump (film), 159, 216–217
48 Days to the Work You Love (Miller),
  155, 222
Freeman, Ronnie, 61–62
Friends, 77, 86–87, 117–118, 185–186
Fulfillment, xiii, xiv
  achievement for, 215, 217
  physical health and, 103–105
  in vocation, 162, 166, 169–170

Gandhi, Mohandas, 62
General Social Survey, 159
Generosity, 181, 184–185
Genetic factors:
  in achievement, 205–208
  in financial decision-making, 181–182
  in health of relationships, 74–76
  in mental and emotional state,
    135–138
  in physical health, 106–108
  in pursuit of purpose, 50–52
  in unique drive, 25–28
  in vocational decision-making,
    156–158
Gift-giving, 56–57
"Glory days," 214
Goals:
  fear of not achieving, 36
  identity shift to pursue, 64
  making the case for not achieving,
    38–39
  for mental state, 145–146

pursuing worthy, 13–17
  risk of not pursuing, 66, 212
  setting realistic, 23–25
Göbekli Tepe, Turkey, 47
Godin, Seth, 65
Gordon, Irving, 105
Graham, Billy, 60
Gratitude, xiii
Greatness, 211
Greenland, 107
Groom, Winston, 217
Guilt, 193

Habits, 12, 115, 120
Happiness, xiv, 17–18
  and achievement, 204
  genetic factors in, 26
  and health/wellness, 116
  and purpose, 48
  relationships and, 71–74, 93
  and religious participation, 51
  in vocation, 163–165
Happiness Pie Chart, 26
Harder, Lori, 101–103, 111, 123
Hardy, Benjamin, 3–9, 11, 13, 102, 117
Harmful activities, drive to undertake,
  13–14
Harvard University, 79, 219
Hatred, of money, 180, 185, 194
"Have to" mindset, 168, 229–237
Health clubs, 126
Health coaches, 126–127
Health span, 120–121
Healthcare spending, 103
Heroes, 49, 68
Hidden drive, 35–36
Hoarding, 181, 184
Homeowners associations, 187
Horie, Kenichi, 104–105, 120
Hulk (Bruce Banner), 16
Human Genome Project, 75
Hunger, 233, 234
The Hunger Project, 32, 49
Hunter, Edward, 28

Identity, 64, 65
Ignorance, of limitations, 210–211
Images of achievement, 219–221
Incentives, 8
Inciting incidents, 4, 7–10, 49
Inclusion, 51
Income (*see* Compensation)
Industrial Revolution, 154
Inspiration, 12–13, 68, 145–146,
  197–198, 214–215, 220

Interconnectedness, 74–75
Interests, purpose and, 62–63
International Mensa Society, 37
Iron Man (Tony Stark), 16, 17
Isolation, 72, 78
It's A Wonderful Life (film), 65–66
"It's All Your Fault" (video), 56
It's Your Call (Barkalow), 218–219
Iyengar, Sheena, 23

James, Randy, 11, 31, 40, 113–115,
    120–121
Jerry Maguire (film), 91–93
Jessica Campbell (Jessica Jones), 16
Job, finding a new, 58, 162
Johansson, Frans, 215
Joneses, keeping up with the, 186–187
Judgment, 57, 212
Justification, 212, 217–218

The Kindness Challenge (Feldhahn), 236
King, Martin Luther, Jr., 62
Korea, 32

Lapin, Daniel, 48, 179–180
Laziness, 12–13
Leach, Robin, 197
Leeper, Mark, 23
Leman, Kevin, 76
*The Life and Strange Surprizing
    Adventures of Robinson Crusoe*
    (Defoe), 22
Life span, 120–121
Lifestyle:
    achievements and, 221
    changing your, 40–41, 113–114, 124
    financial decisions and, 189, 195, 196
    and physical health, 106–109
    vocational decisions and, 160
Lifestyles of the Rich and Famous (TV
    series), 197
Limitless (film), 129–130
Limits:
    on capacity for performance, 130
    ignorance of, 210–211
    and realistic goals, 23–25
    recognizing, xii
    working with limited resources, 21–23
Logic, 35
London School of Economics, 51
Loneliness, 72, 79
Lone-wolf perspective, 93
Longevity, 67
Lottery winners, 195
Love, 49

Love Your Life, Not Theirs (Ramsey), 186
Lyubomirsky, Sonja, 26

MacGyver (TV series), 22
Maker personality type, 33, 34
Making Caring Common Project, 79
Marriage, 81–83, 122
Mars, 212
Mastery, 142–143
The Matrix (film), 64
Meaningful events, 204–205, 216–217
The Medici Effect (Johansson), 215
Medium (platform), 6
Mello, Anthony, 61–62
Mental and emotional state, 129–151
    authentic desires related to, 143–145
    environmental influences on, 138–141
    envisioning yourself improving,
        147–148
    genetic influences on, 135–138
    mental roadblocks to, 141–143
    motives for improving, 145–146
    and potential of the mind, 129–135
    SIDCHAs for, 17–18
    supportive zone for pursuing,
        148–150
Mental fortitude, 124, 142–143, 207
Mental reality, 196–197
Mental roadblocks:
    to achievement, 210–213
    in financial decision-making, 186–189
    to mental and emotional state,
        141–143
    to physical health, 112–116
    to pursuit of purpose, 55–59
    in relationships, 78–90
    in vocational decision-making, 162–165
Mentors, relationship, 97–98
Merton, Thomas, 73–74
Mexican fisherman, parable of, 156–157
Middle Ages, 153
Miller, Dan (dad), 155, 209, 221–222
Miller, Donald, 7, 9, 49
Miller, Jared, 57, 60, 83
Miller, Joanne (mom), 155, 209
A Million Miles in a Thousand Years
    (Miller), 7, 215
Mind:
    connection between body and, 105
    untapped potential of, 129–135
Mind control, 28–29
Mindset, 118, 145–146, 229–237
Minnoch, Jon Brewer, *14*
Money, 153–154, 177–181 (*See also*
    Financial decisions)

The Money Game (radio show), 177
Monogamy, 81, 82
Morals, 29
Motives:
    for achievement, 36, 216–219
    agreement with, 8, 15–16, 61
    behind purpose, 61–63
    as component of unique drive, 34–36
    desire as motivator, 8, 9
    for engaging in relationships, 91–94
    for financial decision-making, 35,
        192–194
    for improving mental and emotional
        state, 145–146
    for improving physical health,
        121–124
    pain as motivator, xiii, 8–9
    for vocational decision-making,
        168–170
Music, 61
My Big Fat Greek Wedding (film), 74–75,
    82, 84

National Basketball Association (NBA),
    24
Natural talent, 163–165, 207, 211
Nature versus nurture debate, 25–26
Negative bias, 138–139
Networking, 173
Neuroplasticity, 50, 142
New York City, 71, 72
No complaint challenge, 235, 236
Nurture personality type, 33
Nutrition (*see* Diet)

Obligation, familial, 85
O'Brady, Colin, 213–214
The Office (TV show), 160
Ohio State University, 221
"Old Friends" (song), 86
Opportunity, money as, 178
Opportunity costs, 119, 188
Outcomes, worthy, 13–17
Overview effect, 83–84
Ownership, 55–56, 121–123, 228,
    233–234

Pain, as motivator, xiii, 8–9, 36, 183
Parents:
    achievements of, 214, 221–222
    financial decision-making by, 182–183
    friendships for, 87
    health and wellness of, 110–111
    influence of, 28–30
    mental/emotional state of, 138–140

    relationships between children and,
        83–84, 92–93, 97–98
    value of relationships for, 74–78
    view of purpose by, 53–54
    vocational decisions of, 159–164, 208
Passion, 59, 149
Passive beliefs, 37
Paul, apostle, 141
Peace, xi, xiv
Peck, Josh, 125
Peloton, 116
Performance:
    authentic desire for, 120
    beliefs and capacity for, 130–134
    financial decisions motivated by,
        192–194
Permission, to achieve, 208, 209
Personal choice, 144, 228, 230–233
Personal gain, 62
Personal rights, 237
Personal trainers, 126–127
Personality tests, 32–34
Peter Parker (Spider-Man), 16
Phenomenon (film), 129
Physical activity, 109–111, 115, 127
Physical health and appearance, 101–128
    achievements related to, 203–204
    authentic desires related to, 118–121
    environmental impact on, 108–112
    envisioning improvement in, 39,
        124–125
    genetic factors in, 106–108
    for Lori Harder, 101–103
    for life fulfillment, 103–105
    mental roadblocks to, 112–116
    motives to pursue, 121–124
    social roadblocks to, 116–118
    supportive zone for pursuing, 125–127
Physical presence, 79–80
Pidgeon, Niyc, 26
Pink, Daniel, 72, 201
Placebo effect, 48
Play, 111, 155–156
Pollan, Michael, 114
Poole, Jennifer, 109
Positive bias, 138–139
Possessions, 189, 191, 193–194
Possibility, 208, 228
Potential, untapped, 129–135
Poverty, 51–52, 182–183, 195
The Power of Regret (Pink), 72, 201
Pride, 61, 62, 65, 118–119, 203–206
Proactive living, 10–13, 227–237
    authenticity in, 234–235
    challenge to undertake, 235–237

extreme ownership in, 233–234
personal choice in, 232–233
reframing reality for, 228–229
and "want to" mindset, 229–237
Proclamation of purpose, 64–65
Proxima Centauri, 212
Purchasing habits (*see* Spending)
Purpose, 47–70
authentic desire to find, 59–60
environmental impact on, 53–54
envisioning your pursuit of, 64–67
faith and, 46–50
genetic impact and, 50–52
of making money, 193
mental roadblocks to, 55–59
motives behind, 61–63
relationships and, 73–74, 79–80, 92
supportive zone for pursuing, 67–68

Ramsey, Dave, 177–178, 185–187
Ramsey, Rachel, 186
Ratey, John J., 138
Reactive living, 10–13, 227
Real, Terry, 135–136, 147, 148, 235
Real estate industry, 119–120
Realistic goals, 23–25
Rebellion, 30, 34, 40, 139, 159
Rector, Ben, 86
Regrets, 72–73, 201–203
Relatability, 148–149
Relationships, 71–98
authentic desires in, 90–91
environmental impact on, 77–78
envisioning your role in, 94–96
genetic drivers of, 74–76
importance of, 71–74
influence of, 40–41
mental roadblocks in, 78–90
motives for engaging in, 91–94
in social groups, 149
supportive zone for healthy, 96–98
Religion, 48, 49, 51, 53
Residual self-image, 64
Resistance, 9–10, 41, 120
Responsibility, 108, 131, 218, 234
Ressler, Kerry, 135
Results, focusing on, 18
Risk, 66, 120, 212
Roadblocks (*see* Mental roadblocks;
Social roadblocks)
Rogers, Woodes, 22
Rohn, Jim, 125, 140
Role models, 145–146, 220–222
Romantic relationships, 81–82, 93–95,
97

Roosevelt, Eleanor, 59
Rwanda, 60

Safety, 178
Scarcity mentality, 56–57, 120, 137,
183–184
The Secret Life of Walter Mitty (film),
202, 215
Secrets of Closing the Sale (Ziglar), 65
Security, 157, 178
Selcraig, Bruce, 21
Self:
relationship with, 80–81, 96–97,
103–104
understanding, 148–149
Self-awareness, 96–97, 166–167, 210–211
Self-compassion, 125, 146, 148
Self-discipline, 40
Self-employment (*see* Entrepreneurs)
Self-image, 118–119, 155, 170–171, 179,
192–195
Self-imposed daily challenging activities
(SIDCHAs), 17–18
Self-interest, 121
Selfishness, 48, 49
Selflessness, 61–62
Selkirk, Andrew, 21–22
Serebriakoff, Victor, 36–37, 130–134
Service, 53, 54, 59–60, 62
Set point, 50–52, 78, 79, 158, 181
Sexual relationships, 81–83
Sharma, Robin, 80
Shatner, William, 83
"Should," motives based on, 122
SIDCHA (blog), 17
SIDCHAs (self-imposed daily
challenging activities), 17–18
Single, remaining, 81–82, 91
Sky burial ritual, 47
Smaller accomplishments, building on,
215
Snake and stick syndrome, 138
Social capital, 154–155
Social conformity, 39–41, 117
Social groups, 87–88, 126, 148–149,
198–199
Social media, 86, 186–187
Social roadblocks to physical health,
116–118
Social status, 185–186, 190, 192–194
Social support (*see* Supportive zone)
Society, meaning of money in, 177–181
Socioeconomic status, 189, 195
Solitude, 73–74, 76
Southern Baptist church, 53

Spark (Ratey), 138
Sparktype, 33, 90
Spending, 186–188, 190–191, 193
Spider-Man (Peter Parker), 16
Spirituality, 47–49, 51, 64
Spodek, Joshua, 17
Stearman, Scott and Hermine, 92–93
Steele, Richard, 22
Stress, 138
Substitutions, dietary, 114–115
Supportive zone:
    for achievement, 221–223
    for changing mental/emotional state,
      140, 148–150
    for financial decision-making,
      197–199
    for healthy relationships, 96–98
    for pursuing physical health,
      125–127
    for pursuing purpose, 67–68
    for vocational decision-making,
      172–174
Survival, necessities of, 178–179
The Swiss Family Robinson (film), 22

Teachers, 139–140, 159, 163
Teresa, Mother, 32, 62
Threat, change as, 41, 126
Tony Stark (Iron Man), 16, 17
The Top Five Regrets of the Dying (Ware),
    72
Tracy, Brian, 222
Trade shows, 198
Training, 133–134, 142
Traumatic upbringing, 25, 85
Trucks, Anthony, 64
Trust, 139
The 12-Hour Walk (O'Brady), 213
Twist, Lynne, 32, 49

Unique drive, your, 21–43
    assembling, 41–42
    belief component of, 36–37
    desire component of, 30–34
    environmental component of, 28–30
    genetic component of, 25–28
    impact of limited resources on, 21–23
    motivational component of, 34–36
    setting realistic goals, 23–25
    and social conformity, 39–41
Unlikely Candidates, 55
Us (Real), 147, 235
US Army, 106–107

US Centers for Disease Control, 103
Utility, as motive, 192–194

Value, of achievements, 60, 202–205
Values, xiii, 29, 146
Vardalos, Nia, 74–75
Verbal thinking, 219
Victim mentality, 28, 55–56, 58–59, 185,
    229–231, 237
Victimization, 55, 58, 231
Virtual environments, 13–14
Vocational decisions, 153–175
    authentic desires in, 166–168
    environmental influences on, 159–162
    envisioning better, 168–172
    exposure as factor in, 31
    feelings about, 155–156
    financial and, 165, 166, 169–170
    and financial decisions, 190
    genetic influences on, 156–158
    historical perspective on, 153–154
    mental roadblocks in, 162–165
    mental/emotional state and, 136–137
    motives for making, 168–170, 192–193
    risk taking in, 120
    supportive zone for, 172–174

Waking up, proactive mindset about,
    236
Walmart, 195
Walton, Sam, 195, 196
"Want to" mindset, 229–237
Ware, Bronnie, 72, 201
Warrior (film), 145
Washington Bullets, 24
Wealth, 156–157, 183, 189–190, 195–197
Weight Watchers (WW), 116, 126
White lies, "have to" mentality in,
    234–235
Williamson, Marianne, 211
Willink, Jocko, 233
Willpower, 40, 112, 115, 117–118
Willpower Doesn't Work (Hardy), 7, 117
Win-win scenarios, 62, 184
Wise Adult, 147–148, 235
Work and workplace, 76, 109, 230–231
    (*See also* Vocational decisions)
World Class Athlete Program, 106–107
WW (Weight Watchers), 116, 126

Zero-sum game (*see* Scarcity mentality)
Ziglar, Zig, 12–13, 65, 222
The Ziglar Show (podcast), 235

ABOUT THE AUTHOR

Kevin is a former pro cyclist, respected peak performance and self-help guide, top-ranking host of the *Self-Helpful* podcast, published author, and father of nine who has devoted himself to helping people remove the barriers to their personal growth and fulfillment. He writes and podcasts amid spending time with his family and running and riding along the high Rocky Mountains trails where they built a big, funky straw bale house in a national forest at 9,200 feet above sea level in the rarified air. Connect with him on social media or at his website, kevinmiller.co.